CUTTING LOOSE
*A Civilized Guide for
Getting Out of the System*

CUTTING LOOSE

*A Civilized Guide for
Getting Out of the System*

DOROTHY KALINS

Saturday Review Press · New York

*Published simultaneously in Canada by
Doubleday Canada Ltd., Toronto.*

Library of Congress Catalog Card Number: 72–88656

ISBN 0–8415–0230–7

Saturday Review Press
380 Madison Avenue
New York, New York 10017

PRINTED IN THE UNITED STATES OF AMERICA

Design by Tere LoPrete

For the Jimmy

Contents

1	Can You Get Out?	3
2	What's Wrong?	17
3	People on the Verge	26
4	The Decision	34
5	Where to Go?	40
6	See America First	60
7	Communes and Homesteading	82
8	The New Work Ethic	107
9	Service Professions	118
10	Money	135
11	Alternate Wife-Styles	147
12	Second Thoughts and Paranoia	157
13	What If You Fail?	173
14	Travel Folders of the Movement	186
	Bibliography	196

CUTTING LOOSE

A Civilized Guide for
Getting Out of the System

I

Can You Get Out?

Left a good job in the city,
Workin' for the man ev'ry night and day,
And I never lost one minute of sleepin',
Worryin' 'bout the way things might have been.*

Getting out is really the cultural opposite of being in. It has been said before, but it's worth repeating, that there are no more provincial thinkers than urban dwellers. Chicagoans have always suffered enough of an inferiority complex as the second city that they might, through humility, gain insight. New Yorkers, however, always have had serious doubts whether there really is life beyond the Hudson. The Mediamakers have charming little catchwords like "the hinterlands" for all that country out there where people can't really live, laugh, or think anything significant. They keep telling themselves and you, "I know what is *really* happening. I am where it's at." To leave convictions like that you have to divest them of importance. Like changing religions, old values must be defused, routed out. You must come to believe that being in

---
* "Proud Mary," J. C. Fogarty, © 1968 Jondora Music.

is not In. Or, if it is, that being where it's at just doesn't matter anymore. It's not that you stop thinking or reading or meeting people. It's that once you're out, the thinking and reading and meeting is not where the action is, except in the house of the volunteer firemen. If you can't take that, you'll never leave. And that's okay too.

Stories about a corporate executive who left New Canaan and moved to Maine become important when you see his counterparts leaving Shaker Heights and Scarsdale and Sausalito and places much less notorious. Moves like this soon make a movement—from all this country's middle-class Thingdoms of comfort and complacency to the few small towns and rural places left where style of life is not so important as the living of it.

There are many people for whom retirement, or children grown, or a great deal of money form a natural breaking point in the process of their lives. For people like this, the leap is not so great. They evolve out of business—it is not a self-generated move that damns the consequences. If they don't have to work out of economic necessity, the chances they take have less risk. They don't *have* to succeed at whatever new venture they choose. These safer people are not the subjects of this book.

Neither are the writers, nor the painters, nor the musicians, whose talent is their baggage and whose only struggle is to decide where on earth to set it down. People who get out became accountants and managers and engineers because they were told early in their lives that they could never make a living as writers or painters or musicians.

Businesswomen and successful blacks are less likely to want to get out, because they recently have gotten in.

And the lower classes are generally working for the very things those who get out reject: status, security, and a lot of cocktail parties.

I know what you're thinking as you sit down with this book: "Look, don't tell me all these stories about corporate vice-presidents who, one day, standing in the middle of Grand Central Station, decide they've had it with the rat race so they go home and pack up the family and sell their house in New Canaan and move somewhere where they run an inn and live happily ever after." I know. You can pick up practically any newspaper these days and read about similar situations.

You don't care too much about the ad guy from New Canaan. You want to know if *you* can do it. Get out. Live a different way, closer to your head and the sweet simple times you knew when you were a kid and things could still make an impression on you. Before you became so used to civilization's atrocities that your only reaction is "that's life."

But secretly *you* suspect That's Not Life. You are too caught up in doing a good and sometimes satisfying job for someone else's ultimate business. Too used to seeing your family through the veil of activity heirs are heir to. You probably believe that things are so complex the old answers won't work because the old questions aren't being asked. And you feel the urge to get back in control of your life. Can you do it?

This book is set up to follow the gradual decision-making steps people go through to get out. All along the way are questions you can ask yourself to gauge your real feelings. You can discover how tied you are to a city/suburb, to a demanding professional-business-corpo-

rate mode, to institutions, to the stimulation and the
money, to Bloomingdale's and Marshall Field—to the
American Dream.

Could you learn, for example, to live without a dozen
movie houses to choose from and as many TV stations?
Can you do without Chinese food at 1 A.M.; fat and
happy lunches at fine French restaurants? Could you
pass up a deal with movers and shakers you meet at dinner parties? Can you bear not knowing what really happened at *The New York Times* because your lawyer knows
their lawyer? Could you lose track of the season at the
theater, not hire the hot interior designer, and stop
buying clothes at wholesale? Can you do without meeting
the mayor? The System is the Big Apple and it feeds on
itself. Can you just toss it away?

"I know what this book is about," said a very tough
New York businessman. "Quitters. Dropouts. Cop-outs."
He spat the words with the disdain of a player who sees a
lot of the best men leaving the game.

There *is* a small group of people who just wander off
somewhere. Robert S. Gallagher wrote a very good book
called *"If I had it to do over again . . ."* about people who
trade in their identities for a chance to escape. Adult
dropouts who, one fine day, walk out on their families,
jobs, and even their names and never come back. Gallagher's dropouts have not gotten out. Nor have the highway hoboes fresh from a middle-class education who, if it
were the fifties, would go pearl diving in the Bahamas,
and today go nowhere. Some people, once undeniably
locked into the system, do wander through life purpose-
lessly as soon as they have made the break. In couples or

alone, they sample communal life, group marriage, strange people, and foreign countries. For these few there is no answer yet. They don't have much to tell us.

The Gotten Out—people who leave the corporate system—leave in families. Most often it is a decision made by a husband worn from the strain of the system. He is middle-class, middle-aged, and whether he will make his money in a store, farm, small service business, or a job taken somewhere just to be there, it's the immediate living, not the eventual profit, that counts. His wife, who was long ago told by the corporate society to take her education and stuff it up some charity envelope (voluntarily), sees the possibilities of putting her energies to some personally rewarding work, often with her husband.

The men and women I interviewed across the United States who have gotten out are not financially independent. The question they answer every step along the way is, "What can I do to earn a living?" Rejection of the system comes usually through strength, not bitterness. "The system," a Wyoming hosteler repeatedly pointed out, "is what gave me the equity in a house in Cleveland that I could sell to start this hostel in the first place." It also gave him skills—amorphous to be sure, but marketing, merchandising, promoting, sales, retailing, engineering, accounting, public relations, banking, brokering, publishing, management do not impede getting out. Rejecting the values of *haute civilisation* doesn't mean not working. As Don Wright, a New Mexico jewelry maker, ex of advertising, ex of academe, says, "If you develop skills as a life-enriching experience, you don't have to be a do-nothing to be free." For the children of the twenties and

thirties and even the forties, who teethed on zwieback
and the work ethic, getting out probably means working
harder. Much harder, but for themselves.

The work they choose often means doing the whole
job, not part of it. The concreteness of the tasks is significant: running a store, a restaurant, a small newspaper, a hotel, chartering yachts, or renting cars. In every
case, the scope of the job is not exceeded by the people
available to do it—the man and whatever members of his
family he can enlist.

It may look like a cop-out from complexity. I don't
think it is. By moving out of the glutted cities and the be-
sotted suburbs into the small and rural towns of this
country, the Gotten Out are putting their intelligence
and their wit and their energy to work in social situations
where they immediately see the results. It is not a return
to the small times of small-town America in the nineteenth century. These emigrés from the city are not
trying to get back to where they once belonged. They
bring to whatever new life they choose all the expertise
and sophistication of their former business and professional lives.

Bob Ballard was deep into the suburban life in Chap-
paqua, New York, managing a $12-million yearly ad
budget for Nestlé's. Now, in his general store in Weston,
Vermont, he uses all the promotional knowledge that
comes from years on Madison Avenue. When he sells
Wisconsin instead of Vermont cheese, it's not Wisconsin
per se, but "from a little dairy west of here." He keeps a
wood stove burning all year because skiers like the smell,
even though it is no longer the only source of heat. He
grinds up pounds of coffee, far more than he sells, be-

cause that, too, smells like a general store should. A seventy-two-year-old butcher comes in three times a week because "he looks like he belongs here." Each room in the old rambling building has its own street entrance and distinctive name and sign, based on Ballard's conviction that people will think they're in a different store and therefore spend more money. Still, this is really only a small-town operation. Besides tourists, there are about only 500 people in Weston, Vermont.

The Gotten Out, by moving on in with their city-slickered ways, just may validate and invigorate the little places—provide an alternate way for an educated, intelligent person turned on by life to live.

One of the Above

To research this book, I traveled to many of the places in this country where people go to get out. I interviewed scores of people in their new lives, had letters and tapes from many more. While every one of these people had a great story to tell, to recount them all here would become repetitious and dulling. You read one case history, . . . etc. So here is one case history. Not a composite character built from the experiences of many, but the real flesh and blood of the Movement. His points of indecision and hesitation are similar to those of others trying to get out; his eventual commitment and dedication are also very much the same.

Miles Turnbull was smaller than most other farm boys of the rural Midwest, but that probably made him a lot smarter—a personality kid. After the requisite years on the upward trail—state university in journalism, publishing and sales promotion—Miles found himself Midwestern marketing director for *Successful Farming* magazine in 1969. He managed the Chicago office with three salesmen working for him. He lived with his wife and the predictable two children, one of each kind, in the suburb of Evanston. "Wedded to the capitalist life, but uneasy. I mean how can you tell your kid you're a space salesman and expect him to understand what you do?"

The unrest was familiar. In 1964 after he had married his wife, Jane, an advertising copywriter, they tried to get out, to buy a small newspaper, the *Hungry Horse News*, in Columbia Falls, Montana. "But then Jane got pregnant and we chickened out. We thought, 'If we ever couldn't afford it, it was now.' We thought we'd have to give the baby a nice home. So we were older and wiser and opted for security. And we got deeper and deeper into the metropolitan thing that we had grown to distrust and dislike. But we were very much entrenched in the corporate life.

"Then, five years later, in the winter of 1969, we got a letter from the guy at the *Hungry Horse News*, sounding us out again. He suggested that we were too much 'in' to think about getting out now. That letter was a challenge. I wrote him a cautious reply and began to think, 'Wait a minute, just how wedded to security are you?' It's funny how the idea works on you. Once you get it in your head, you begin to notice every irritation of urban living. The first thing to get to me was the shuffling at Union Station. Shuffle, shuffle. Here are all these cats making all this money and still they shuffle like everyone else. Shuffle, shuffle. Pretty soon that's all you can hear. Then, I'd sit in my high-rise office overlooking Monkey Ward's a few blocks away. And soon I couldn't see Ward's anymore because of this yellow curtain of pollution and I thought, 'Beyond that curtain are my kids and they're breathing this stuff.'

"You have to ask yourself, 'Why are you really doing this?' Are you running to, or away from. I couldn't tell. I mean we're certainly normal. We're not running from society if you know what I mean. [I do. He means they're relatively straight, short of hair, and more conventional of purpose than the middle-aged hippie who drops out to stalk the peyote weed.] You look harder into your heart and you try to see if you're copping out—and how much corporate security you have to give up. You have to weigh that against the lack of personal involvement and identity we felt in Chicago.

"Every morning when I looked at myself in the mirror I asked, 'Okay, Miles, you're forty years old. What do you want to be when you grow up?'

"So Jane and I thought about the small-town newspaper business. The longer we thought, the more picky we got. We liked that guy's Montana newspaper, but we didn't like his rain. We figured if we were going to do this, we wanted mountains, a climate with plenty of sunshine, no humidity, not too cruel a winter nor too hot a summer. We thought of the Southwest, Wyoming and Montana and western Colorado, feeling that eastern Colorado will soon be a megalopolis. One day I got *Ayer's Directory of Publications* and wrote twenty-seven letters of inquiry to newspapers. I was pretty specific about my credentials and financial situation. I knew I couldn't afford to buy anything outright, but I didn't want them to think I was some guy who got drunk one afternoon and decided to go West. We got thirteen answers.

"That summer we decided to go on a wilderness trip to get mountain fever out of our systems. We were afraid that the first mountain we saw with a newspaper under it we'd buy. We hadn't even thought of Utah, but the broker explained it was right next to Colorado. We both knew when we drove out of Monticello, Utah, that we would come back to the *San Juan Record*."

Said Miles. Jane was frightened. "I was afraid my parents [her father was a professor at the law school of the University of Missouri] would think we were out of our minds. Sure, I didn't like Evanston—we were tied to our little house on our little block in our little over-priced neighborhood—it used to take an hour and a half in the grocery store. But I was scared. There were many ogres, we didn't know anyone. We had no idea what we were getting our kids into. I knew my life would change because I'd be working with Miles on the paper. I couldn't make a decision. I cried a lot. Miles tried not to press me, but one day he got fed up and said, 'Okay, Jane, when are you going to make up your mind?' Finally I agreed."

Then there was the telling to be done. Jane's friends were a little shocked and confessed they couldn't leave the shopping. "You're going to a town of 14,000," they said in horror. "No, no," Jane would correct, "1400." Miles's boss was "sympathetic—a little envious maybe."

"We lost a lot of money on the house," Miles says, "but if we had been held up by money we never would have left. A person who is going to hold on to every cent of equity is never going to see the other side of the mountain."

They bought the *San Juan Record* with a small down payment and lots of help from the friendly local bank.

Monticello, Utah, has a wide main street where at any time there are more pickup trucks than cars. It's a Mormon town, on the edge of the Navaho Nation, surrounded by the San Juan Mountains. In the motel room at Hall's Triangle H are the following books: *Positive Christian Living*; *The Book of Mormon*; *Steps to Christ*; *A Day to Remember*, compliments of the Seventh-Day Adventists; *The Desire of Ages*, with a Christ by Norman Rockwell's impostor on the cover. On the wall, Navaho by way of Greenwich Village, is an oil painting on black velvet of an Indian woman, gray hair held back with a hippie's headband, a string of turquoise beads on her sunken chest.

"The paper hit rock bottom the day we moved in," Miles says. "The major advertiser dropped out. I knew it was a sick operation, but I didn't know it was dying. The previous owner had filled the pages with canned crap. He stopped covering Monticello's neighbor/rival Blanding. There was no goodwill left.

"I experienced post partum depression of sorts. Cutting the cord from the corporation is not unlike leaving the womb. It was a shock when I first realized that nobody was going to send us a paycheck, that our money depended on what I did with this business this day. I was depressed, but really depressed. We rented this small apartment across the street from the newspaper office and I would wake up at 4 A.M., pounding the pillow and screaming, 'Jane, I can't do it.'

"But somehow I did. I found selling the same whether it's the Chicago big time or a page in the newspaper. A

small-town newspaperman is more salesman than jour-
nalist anyway. Old Vint was the big advertiser who
dropped out. Now I can't just go and lean on Old Vint,
I've got to have the numbers."

Besides the paper, the Turnbulls do job printing and
run a stationery supply business from part of the newspaper office, which means taking time away from writing a
story to sell eighteen cents worth of file folders or a nickel
envelope. And what kind of job printing does a small-
town paper do? One hundred posters that say "We think
Father Spellan is great!" for a group of churchgoers who
want to defend their priest who was badmouthed because
it was alleged he abetted an affair between a youth
worker and a local matron.

"We can't afford the people who would let us go to bed
early, so we work late every night and stay up all night
Wednesday to get the paper out on Thursday." Jane is
losing the suburban urge to keep her apartment spic and
span, so little is she in it. "It's a mama and papa operation just like the old grocery stores. The kids are learning
how a newspaper works. If we're lucky and stay on this
property, we just may start getting it paid off by the time
we start paying for college. But we don't care about dollars as dollars. I know that even if we go stark-staring
bankrupt we did the right thing.

"You know, there were guys who said, 'Ah, the desert
island,' when we told them we were leaving Chicago. But
if one of those guys came out here today and said, 'Ah,
the desert island,' I'd punch him in the nose, after the
hard work and seriousness with which we approach this."

Miles and Jane have rejuvenated the *San Juan Record*.

As one unusually articulate fan letter said, "We can call you revivalists or just plain magicians. Overnight you have transformed pix into pictures." The pictures Miles takes himself, always with humorous quip-captions. Hometowny, you betcha. Each week the logo is another photograph of local scenery, pretty mountains, or pretty girls with the tag ". . . another wonder of San Juan County."

Miles puts on a little country boy himself, throwing in an "ain't" here and there in a mock dialect and purposely misusing grammar, which is a bit strange for a journalism graduate. In a short front-page piece explaining poor television reception for the area, he wrote:

> What happened was, the relay tower on the mountain, probably overladen with ice, blew over, and with it went "As the World Turns." . . . I can tell you it was no "Secret Storm" what done it. It was that superhowler we had about ten days ago.

"I knowingly don't cover things that a daily wouldn't be caught dead not covering," he explains. "If someone came up to me and said, 'Hey, they declared World War III,' I'd say, 'Fine, I'll try to get it in next week.' You become so wrapped up with the lives in the county that's all that matters. I've got to have the human events. Kids and dogs and Little League baseball and scenery, and if I miss a city council meeting, I don't lose sleep over it.

"The satisfaction I get from this newspaper—I can reach out and touch it, and what's more I can remember writing it and pasting it up. I am that newspaper and

that newspaper is us. Sure you get fanatical. You get fanatical about every little detail. But that's the great
thing. Here you're the head fanatic."

A recent issue of the *San Juan Record* announced the result of a gutsy circulation drive that raised the readership
a third. On the same page, a little notice: "We are
finding working all night Wednesday a little wearing,
and we figure this [the closing of the office on Wednesday
afternoons] might be a way to shorten the working
night."

There's the NU VU Drive-In movie in Monticello,
Utah, but the Turnbulls don't go much. Their office is
the center of their social life—what few local business
friends they have managed to make often come to see
them there. It's a long way from the Evanston cocktail
circuit. Their most frequent visitor is the chief of police,
who spends his night duty over the *Record*'s coffee pot.
Miles and Jane are the only other people up on a Monticello night, and that includes criminals.

On a rare free evening, Miles and Jane will grab a
couple of sandwiches and drive up the nearby mountain,
past the piece of land they'd like to build a house on, one
day. It's a ten-minute route with literally dozens of deer
leap-leaping out of the road. They eat their sandwiches
to the fading light as the sun slips behind a mountain
range they can see almost fifty miles away. Up here they
find all the answers—why they left. And why they'll
never go back.

2

What's Wrong?

The first time they picked the lock. The second time they just took it out altogether. I knew my original locks were weak—I picked them myself once when I forgot my keys. . . . Now I'm a veteran. I can tell stories at parties along with the rest of them. I've paid my psychological dues for living in Manhattan. I think about getting out, but where could I run to?

A young male tenant, *Life*, November 19, 1971

"Rat race" is a term taken from the early days of experimental psychology, when those normally slow-paced rodents were ripped from their natural habitat and placed on a laboratory treadmill to perform. Activity, never mind what kind, was its own reward. Those rats, in competition with each other, and thanks to B. F. Skinner, were taught reinforcement and chaining. Each sequence of activity was properly rewarded—a paycheck, if you will. I was surprised to hear the worn old term "rat race" used so frequently in describing what it was people wanted to get away from. It has become its own cliché—perhaps because it's true. Many of us have been exposed to just enough behavioral psychology to be able to pull away and observe our activity as so much learned response. Scurrying around on someone else's corporate jungle gym, telling yourself you must be going places because you're always finding yourself in strange airports.

Routine for its own sake is experienced on all levels, not only big-city corporate maneuvering. An insurance salesman in rural Illinois complained to me, "Every day getting up and doing the same thing, just to make enough money. The pressures, they get you down." The syndrome begins to seem incredible. Here is this salesman driving around the flatlands of Illinois, watching the primary greens and golds of crops butt up against a distant horizon, and he thinks he's in a rat race? "It's *having* to sell insurance all day. Pretty soon you forget about the country and you grind your gut about making a sale. A guy I knew just quit it all and bought an old railroad station in southern Iowa, and he's going to make candles for a living. Now that's a living."

The rat race describes mindless activity. The participants are likable enough, there in their gray flannel suits—updated in subtle windowpane checks, suppressed waists, and at least two vents. In the 1950s, "The Man in the Gray Flannel Suit" was invincible. I can remember when they were shooting the movie. Gregory Peck, his suit as ritualistic as medieval armor, a Thomas Begg hat on his head, brandished his briefcase and hallowed the sidewalks of Westport with his cordovans. He was sophistication, suburban suave, trading well-turned phrases with his look-alikes at the station, waiting for the 7:37. In those days, the train station at 7:37 was the big time.

The irony is that the writer who made the Man and his Suit a symbol of an age has himself gotten out. Sloan Wilson, in a book written in 1969 called *Away from It All*,

describes feelings that led him to buy a boat and run
away to sea:

> In the suburbs I had, one after the other, owned
> seven houses and had somehow contrived to be mis-
> erable in all of them. . . . Much to my alarm, I was
> growing fat, which is a terrible thing to happen to a
> man who also has to carry more than the normal
> load of vanity.

Drinking too much, divorce, Vietnam, "friends who
seemed even more backbiting, joyless and hysterically
critical of each other than is usual for a literary set," and
primarily, "the fact was that with increasing speed not
only I but the world seemed to be going mad, and I
wanted to get the hell out of it as far as possible."

Somewhere in the sixties, coupled with an increasingly
acute social consciousness, The Man in the Gray Flannel
Suit—Suburbman—ceased to be an idol. And although
men continued to mass at railroad stations as they do
today, commuting is an indignity to be borne. A
wretched connection of the rush of the city to the hush of
the bedroom town.

Suburbmen, obsessed with commuting, figure out just
how much of their semiawake lives the going and coming
takes. A familiar figure is the total of seven or eight weeks
a year. Measuring out their lives in coffee spoons. Plastic.
And the coffee is "to go."

There's a cartoon going round consisting of a ballot
that directs "Check one: Bang ☐ Whimper ☐." Some
say "fire"; others, "race riots." What's wrong is pounded
dully into our heads with every issue. Even casual con-

versations give rise to a nauseous feeling of powerlessness.
We can't do anything about it.

Echoes of what's wrong kept following me throughout
this research. At a casual Cambridge dinner one night, a
young Harvard professor of social psychology predicted
with humorless finality that the next decade will see the
center cities totally occupied by blacks, kept in, com-
pressed by the surrounding rings of white middle-class
suburbs. It will create, he says, a concentration of tension
that can't help but explode. Some days later, at a similar
dinner, an economist friend envisioned the next few years
when our dollar has been devalued to twenty cents and
says, "There is nothing we've ever lived through to de-
scribe what it will be like, not even the depression.
Maybe the South during Reconstruction tells it best,
when there was no money and what there was couldn't
buy anything." Dresses made from tablecloths and dra-
peries. We never thought a time would come when the
money in our savings banks wouldn't be safe. It depends
on whose prophecies of doom you want to believe. But
even the giddily optimistic Charles Reich *(The Greening of
America)* rationalizes his hedge against demise in an interview in *Rolling Stone*:

> Let's put it this way. Supposing for a moment that
> the vision [his new consciousness] is a mistake.
> What have we to look forward to: the police state,
> fascism, sterile art? So why not let's have the vision?

Predicting disaster may be fashionable. The current
response is the dumb smile face ☺ , which people stick
to car bumpers and refrigerators. When confronted with

overwhelming, often irrational complexity, the reaction is ☺ . "Things aren't really all that bad" is the insipid message.

We live in a time when the anonymous treacheries of Ma Bell and the power utilities mean not temporary breakdown but wholesale crumbling of the system. Not everyone who leaves the corporate life does so as the one, perfect, existential act against the system—an affirmation of the self. A philosophical weight that strong would prohibit retrenchment, which everyone who gets out, admit it or not, builds into his plans. (Many who have gotten out still depend on the system for livelihood.) But the act of getting out is heavily symbolic just the same. The raising of one small fist. (Right off.) And perhaps the only creative way man has left to spit in the eye of the prophet of doom.

The urban media, in a semimasochistic way, become fascinated with the people who reject what it stands for. Print and television have done a lot to feed the Movement. Listen to this ad for *Harper's Bazaar*:

> When the Hamptons
> seem endless.
> Connecticut too easy.
> St. Tropez too expected.
> It's time for
> a Bazaar adventure.

Are they kidding? With a case of twentieth-century malaise that bad, no magazine can help. The media are full of getting-out tales:

The New York Times describes a man named Al Hartig,

who left his job at a decorative accessories factory in the Bronx to make kites on Nantucket's South Wharf. "It was a growing lack of joy. A lack of trust." The dehumanizing effects of life in New York. "I realized I wouldn't even rescue a cat off an awning any more."

Jim Stingley, writing in the *Los Angeles Times*, did one of the first and most convincing pieces of journalism about people getting out to Bozeman, Montana. He quotes a precision machinist from Phoenix, Arizona, who took a janitor's job for less than half pay in Bozeman just to be there: "The smog. And I wanted to give my kids a chance to live without all this dope." And a Los Angeles salesman: "You know I don't think my children have a future there. A negative psychological effect prevails on them and I don't think any kids in Los Angeles have much hope."

David Susskind, that sometime and onetime barometer of social change, had a ninety-minute show called "City Slickers Head for the Sticks" and was incredulous throughout (as befits a New Yorker) that these people could really exist out of the city. "What do you do at night?" he kept asking. "What happens in the winter?" One of his guests, Robert Alan Arthur, was a writer who had moved to East Hampton, Long Island, certainly Manhattan's backyard if it ever had one. But to the irrepressible Susskind, even that was getting out.

"It was amazing," said another guest, Mike Mitchell, a Wall Street insurance broker who now runs an inn in Maine. "David kept insinuating, first that there must be something wrong with me—then, that I must be running away from something. If I was running away from any-

thing, it was more success and money. To David, there seemed something un-American in that."

Throughout the scenario of the Gotten Out are dramatic, repentant stories of lives lived wrong. Men saying they used to spend more money on liquor in one week than they now spend on groceries for a month. Every day, reformed petty philanderers take their once obscenely acquisitive wives and cleanse themselves in the spare, thrift air of a new life. For these sultans of suburbia, the error of their ways could be shown in one of those superwide-angle photographs of everything you can buy with Master Charge. Acquisition is one kind of self-evaluation that is often mistaken for success. "Well," a man will say, "I'm doing pretty well. I live in a $65,000 house. We get two brand-new cars every year, I'm a member of the golf and tennis club, so I must be doing okay."

In motel rooms across the country are little placards conscientiously put there by the phone company to remind traveling men of their tenuous relationships with their families. There is a picture of a wife with a Jane Powell hairdo sitting in an armchair by the phone, surrounded by her children, suburban waifs. "Call us," they plead with eyes large and wet with waiting. "Find time every day to be alone, if only for a few minutes with your wife and each child," instructs a memo to corporate executives from Washington University's Graduate School of Business. "If you can't be home, telephone and talk to all members of your family."

If such is the inhumanity of the corporate state, there's small wonder at a man who will throw it all over for a little love. "I'm ashamed to admit I never talked to my children before we moved up to Vermont," a former advertising agency vice-president confessed to *The Wall Street Journal.*

"Money doesn't buy happiness" we all say but don't really believe. Ann and Bruce Glenn's story has all the morality of Aesop. Before they got out of New York for their summer-turned-year-round house on a little island off Rhode Island, Bruce was head of the design department at Bobbie Brooks, a large clothing corporation. As Ann tells it, "Before we left the city we were living on 66th Street between Third and Lexington in a fabulous seven-room apartment surrounded on three sides by terraces and views. Bruce was going to work around eight and not coming home till seven-thirty. He never saw our daughter Christina and rarely saw me, alone at any rate. We were home maybe three nights out of seven. We were always going to Museum of Modern Art openings, Metropolitan Opera openings, Lincoln Center openings (members of all), Broadway show openings, fund-raising parties, etc. Clothes and personal appearance took a great deal of my time. I had been a model before I married Bruce, and with his being in the fashion business, I thought it necessary to uphold some kind of image. The rest of my time was spent 'busying' myself taking courses on antiques, lunching with friends and decorating part-time. I saw very little of our daughter. We always had a live-in maid, rented limousines, owned a Lincoln, and for a while even had a houseman and chauffeur.

"Bruce was making lots of money, but we were spending lots of money doing all the 'right' things—living in a super apartment, me wearing $600 dresses, probably spending $5000 a year just at the hairdressers. What is one working for? Happiness or accumulating money? Neither was happening to Bruce."

For him, the special thrill of a fashion life was "hollow, false, and really a large put-on. To spend your whole life at that is wasteful." Before they left, Bruce had found some sort of salvation at the potter's wheel, which gradually wore away his frustration and miserable sense of self. In Rhode Island, the Glenns run a crafts center where Bruce can work every day and a country store that Ann manages seven days a week.

The Glenns are part of an increasing number of people who can't get no satisfaction going after and getting the things they're supposed to want.

3

People on the Verge

Nathaniel Hawthorne was getting out of Boston, Massachusetts, in the 1840s to Brook Farm, the famous experiment in living, and later wrote in *The Blithedale Romance*:

> We had broken through many hindrances that are powerful enough to keep most people on the weary tread-mill of the established system, even while they feel its irksomeness almost as intolerably as we did.

Many people today feel the irksomeness of the system—almost as intolerably as Hawthorne did. But they're somehow incapable of doing anything about it.

At least for now. Instead, they talk about it. For some, the hindrances that keep them on the treadmill are obvious: they are obsessed with Making It, even though they like to talk as if they aren't. Others cling to an identity their business role gives them, even if it's also doing them in.

One friend who has a good job with New York City's Addiction Services Agency called and said, "Every time I pass a globe I find myself leaning towards it. I keep walking into foreign airline offices just to smell the air." This same man put an ad in *The Wall Street Journal* that read: "Young executive willing to leave secure, high-paying job for interesting and worthwhile experience. . . ."

Another friend insists he is only minutes away from taking off. First, he took me down to see a barge on the Saugatuck River that he was thinking of hauling up to Martha's Vineyard to live, Gulley Jimson style, in the water off some land he owned. Then it became a kind of ark for his son, Noah. The plan was to roll it onto the land and use it as a base for a house. The barge was forsaken, however, for a barn he's building on the property, with thoughts of taking off any minute now. Meanwhile, though, he has a very important job in network television that he wouldn't want jeopardized by revealing his name.

Almost everyone walking the streets of some big city has a contingency dream he's working on. A furniture designer I know keeps figuring out ingenious new ways to build a mythical house that someday will succor him from the cruel world. One month he plans it in the Ozarks, the next, Maine.

"Just you wait," a couple with a thirty-foot boat keep

telling me. "One day we're going to take this baby out and never come back. Open up a shipyard in Barbados. Live on the boat." Who knows? It's been done. But whether this guy will leave an advertising business that keeps rewarding him with higher numbers and longer hours, and whether his wife will ever give up a job with an airline that sends them ever so many places for ever so little. Stick around.

Another couple living just outside of Cambridge, Massachusetts, have more philosophical/romantic visions. They want to go to a small community with harsh living conditions, wicked weather, so they can feel the spirit of community. "Nova Scotia," they say, "is fast being bought up by Americans." Though they've never been there, they've *almost* decided to pit their energies against the basic living condition.

It is interesting that wives of men who contemplate getting out—and many of them are professionals themselves—do not resist the move as much as their husbands. Perhaps because even the younger ones were told to have jobs that could be complementary to their anticipated husbands. They were nudged toward teacher and secretary jobs so that they could easily adapt, move at will. Because these women were socially force-fed a certain lack of ambition themselves (despite achievement in a sealed-off academic environment), many of them feel little identity in a job, and not much more at home. They see that getting out would put them in a position to start again in a different kind of marriage and a new kind of work. In a position there isn't a role definition for.

Younger women are more eager to push their husbands over the verge and out. Older corporate wives are sometimes far too entrenched in the corporate structure themselves to be able to understand, much less encourage, a life change. Too accustomed are they to playing the hierarchies—and bridge—too settled in a world they know and even love.

There is something subtly binding about a corporation's ties to an individual: a person gets his sense of himself, of importance and prestige from the way a company, never particularly noted for humanity, sees fit to evaluate him. He attaches himself to a system of arbitrary reward and anonymous condemnation so remote as to have him constantly insecure and always striving for security. Which is what the company had in mind all along. It is this subtle control over an individual's identity that makes it so difficult to get out. Here is an example of a struggle that's happening now; the story of a man hanging on the verge, caught by a company, both of whose names are better left anonymous.

He graduated with a master's degree from one of the best business schools in the country and afterward got a job with one of the largest public-accounting firms in the world. He was an initiate, automatically put in the bottom slot on teams sent out to audit corporate books all over New York. Petrified by his lack of knowledge, he soon found that he knew just a bit less than his immediate supervisors. By playing the role of a good guy with an unflagging sense of humor, he managed in his first year not to threaten anyone enough to not succeed himself.

The yearly tax-return ritual turned the months of March and April into indistinguishable blurs of overwork and late hours as his team readied its clients to meet the government.

The next year he married and spent a lot more time than he would have liked on New York Central trains. He and his wife had moved from Greenwich Village to an apartment in Riverdale and a magnificent view of the George Washington Bridge. That view was soon totally obstructed by a building of blue tile and glass brick that rose up across the street. His firm's evaluation of him in closed-door sessions with his supervisors was that he was doing quite well and although a promotion was called for, the firm couldn't be pinned down. The few colleagues he liked and respected began leaving and getting fired, and he felt he must be doing something wrong to be kept on like this. But the company meant a lot to him: "I am in this big operation and I'm doing okay," he kept telling himself.

He spent the next year walking into great banks and telling them what they were doing wrong. Sometimes he didn't walk out before midnight. Later that year, he found a bank error of many thousands of dollars, which added to his reputation. Lest he get cocky or complacent, however, the personnel director took one hundred accountants into a room one morning, and when he had finished, none of them had jobs. The great purge put an unfamiliar quake in his step and some lines in his brow as he raced for the 7:05 P.M., or the 8:05 P.M., or the 9:05 P.M. to Riverdale. Or to attend a Savings and Loan Dinner (his wife called them White Socks Balls), where he was careful not to wear his peace-symbol cufflinks or show undue sympathy for minorities, no matter how fashionable. As it was, he had to take enough guff from guys about going to the ballet with his wife instead of bowling.

His daughter was born and he now headed teams auditing manufacturing companies. He often felt put upon that he was given flunkies to work for him—men he would have been ashamed to hire. Was this a reflection on him? The following year with the big promotion still tantalizing—the great seal of approval—he got his first inquiries from headhunters. One rainy night he even went out to meet a man at the airport for a job interview. His wife, wanting for him a quieter, simpler life, surreptitiously investigated the public-accounting market in small towns throughout the country. She, with a master's degree in business herself, felt sure she could find work in research almost anywhere. He didn't want to leave the company, though, without reaching what he thought was a respectable level. He tried to pass the CPA exams twice that year, cramming six-week brush-up courses into a few weekends. He didn't make it.

Later the next winter, after a series of courses taken at a dingy midtown hotel that was surrounded by prostitutes, he finally passed his CPA exams and had three more initials of achievement to put after his name. Brought in for his regular report-card session, his next promotion was hinted at with the merest suggestion that it would be his, except for the objections of a Japanese partner in the firm who had never worked with him, but had misgivings all the same. He fought World War II over and over in his head at night, writhing sleepless for weeks under the scrutiny of the wily Japanese. It was almost summer when he got his promotion in spite of the Oriental. At once he decided he owed the company at least another year, which would give him experience in a management position. He became a supervisor.

It was a strange thing to feel allegiance to this company that expressly refused to do anything to keep its employees. It operated on the triangle theory—to hire a lot of cheap young employees at the bottom, bill them out at high rates, and divide the spoils among the partners at the top, in a caste system that rivaled India's. Indeed, these czar/partners seem to have forfeited their names in the scramble for title and were referred to only as "the partners."

To make partner was a thing he tried not to think of and, instead, made plans to build an entire room onto his parents' summer house. His wife gently told him that if he spent another summer on the house instead of with his family she didn't know what she would do. So they went fishing instead: two weeks of rain and no fish. The rest of the time he worried about smoking so he wouldn't eat too much, or eating so he wouldn't smoke too much.

He slept badly, waking up in the early hours and often unable to sleep again. The doctor he went to told his wife, "Your husband is seriously exhausted."

Early this year I finally asked him what it was that kept him working for the company. "Why can't you just get out?" He thought about it for a while and said, "This might sound a little gross, but it's like making it with a girl for the first time. No matter what your feelings are about her, you know you've got to do it once. And if you set yourself up to make it in a company, you've got to make it to prove to yourself that you can do it."

"But how much do you have to prove?"

"Till you're sure."

4

The Decision

How do people deep in the system finally make the decision to get out? Ironically enough, they first have to succeed at whatever work they are doing. The Gotten Out ward off the accusation of copping out by showing fervent dedication to this other, new way of life. They defy the charge of running away by dragging out their records of success in numbers—past salaries at least twice what they're making now—and great heartfelt endorsements of their previous ways of life. "I love advertising," several men have said. "It's not that I didn't love advertising."

Before a person actually gets out, he must reach a

Level of Achievement in a company. The LOA does not mean earning potential; it means how much you're content to make. The level is initially determined by promotions, but soon it becomes a numbers game. Each person's level is different. Some are content with $25,000 a year. For others, it's $125,000 and out. You can determine yours by starting at the low numbers, say $10,000, and increasing by fives, repeat the succession of numbers over in your head until you reach what you're making now. You'll see that you were not the least bit interested in the smaller numbers, but as they approached your present income, your interest quickened. Then, continue past your income, by fives, and see how long your interest lasts. When you get to the point when one high number doesn't make your heart beat any faster than the next high number, you have passed the Level of Achievement you have implicitly set for yourself. Freedom means reaching an LOA, then losing interest in the numbers game happily ever after.

A successful publishing executive I know seemed mystified by the fact that he was still in the business, though he had been talking for years about buying a small radio station in the country. "I guess things have been happening so fast that I haven't even had time to think about it. I guess that sounds strange," he said, thinking about it. He just hasn't reached his LOA yet.

Calculating your Level of Achievement is one way to get at your future. Another related way is projection—trying to put yourself in your boss's job to see if that would make a positive difference in the quality of your life.

Mont Johnston was a divisional vice-president for Allied Chemical, then promoted to special assistant to the group vice-president. He was commuting three hours and forty minutes a day from Morristown, New Jersey, to the Allied Chemical tower in Times Square. "What," he asked himself on one of those long train rides, "would you do if you were making as much as your boss? I figured it out and it came to four or five thousand dollars more after taxes. That would just buy more things, I thought, and then I saw that I didn't want to buy anything. I wanted the time, not the job, which was not very different from my own." So, even though the numbers on Mont Johnston's scorecard were closer to $100,000 than not, "it was," he realized, "just a scorecard." So, within the year, Mont Johnston left Allied Chemical and with his wife moved to Albuquerque, New Mexico, where he manages an adventurous housing concept called La Luz.

Eugene Foushee, a geologist with Union Carbide, knew that his next step was from Colorado to a glassed-in office in New York City. He says, "I knew that if I was really successful I'd wind up in corporate headquarters, and that's just too far from the geologist's dream of supplying pitchblende to Madame Curie." So he quit Union Carbide and with his wife and baby went to Bluff, Utah, where they opened a coin laundry and lived in it until the motel they built themselves was finished. "Eugene was always talking about getting me to Indian country, but I thought he meant for a weekend," said his wife, Mary, who had expected something more along the lines of an apartment on Park Avenue than a laundromat in Bluff.

When a man gets to the point where he can see that his next promotion is just more of the same; when the idea of greater areas of wall-to-wall carpet and another combination of buzz words that make a title just do not excite him anymore, he has reached his Level of Achievement. Most people are so caught up with the need to succeed, they don't stop and project themselves into the realities of that success. It is a heady freedom to finally see that the prospect of moving up doesn't have the same lure as the possibility of moving out.

But Making It has a pernicious control over even the most independent of us, which is why the public accountant from New York is still on the verge. Disillusionment is far too much with us every day anyway to be a one-time catalyst. The decision isn't made from some sudden, naïve appraisal of a situation, like "this company is very self-serving and bureaucratic and capitalistic and what's more there's no justice or social conscience here, so I'm going to cut off my necktie and just get out."

More potent as a one-time catalyst on the American businessman is the impending age of forty. Somehow forty not only threatens masculinity but it also signals the first day of the rest of one's life. Many people, along with newspaper owner Miles Turnbull, have said, "Okay, kid, what are you going to do with your life now that you're forty?" Several couples have explained that if they were ever going to do it, they had to do it while they were still young. And forty seems to be the magic number for summing up and questioning. "What have I done with my life?" And the optimistic hope I've heard from many: "There must be something better."

Getting out is a little like marriage. Pure joy doesn't necessarily pull you in and intolerable pain doesn't always wrench you out. There are, however, last straws that will clinch a decision all but made. For one man who left Westchester County for Vermont, his last straw was a friend being mugged in New York at 2 A.M. "I knew then that I had reached the threshold of paranoia in dealing with the city and that it would only be worse from then on," he explained. For another, "It was the day I came back from California after six months and I realized suddenly that the defenses a New Yorker builds up—that close out the noise and the dirt, the harassment—I'd let them down. And all at once I was being pounded from all sides. And I got so up tight that I said, 'We're getting out of here.' And I got rid of the place in the city and we took off and that was it."

For an engineer who spent weeks at a time away from his family, alienated from all that he cared about, it was "driving across Nevada. That's a long way to think, and I suddenly realized I couldn't live this lonely way anymore." These last straws must coincide, however, with a certain Level of Achievement attained, or they will be suffered silently and not acted upon.

There is an idea among people on the verge that all they have to do is wait for the right thing to come along and that thing will get them out. In most cases this is not true. Most people find the right thing after the decision has been made. They tell it the same way: "If it wasn't this [restaurant, shop, inn], it would have been something else."

Bob Ballard spent seven years scouring the state of Vermont for a good business to get into, and it was the year he finally "made it" in his own mind that he stumbled onto a general store and wanted it despite the protests of his accountants—the place hadn't grossed more than $2000 the year before.

Mike Mitchell was looking for a boat business and he wound up running an inn. Fred Lesswing thought he'd get into local real estate, and he now owns a hardware store. Colby Wilson was looking for a small weekly newspaper and he started a ski resort. It's not the thing per se, but the time that's right.

5

Where to Go?

Better air to breathe. Air that had not been breathed once and again! air that had not been spoken into words of falsehood, formality, and error, like all the air of the dusky city!
Nathaniel Hawthorne, *The Blithedale Romance*, 1852

Getting out is physical change. Although some couples successfully drop into New York City, fed by welfare, to really get out you have to move. So-called changing careers in middle age is change indeed, and while many of these changes have the requisite slowing of pace and cut in income, where you live is a big part of the problem. The cloak-and-suiter who forsakes the garment district for the Youth Corps in New York, the ex-art director at Hallmark who tries subsistence living in an old Kansas City house heated by firewood gleaned from construction sites, the Minneapolis patent lawyer who starts a minority-operated business making dulcimers, right in the Twin City—all of the above have changed, but they have not gotten out.

Getting out means moving. Back to the land and away from the lawn.

A 1973 Gallup poll showed that 8 out of 10 of America's adult city dwellers would like to live in a less urbanized place if they could. Given a choice of city, suburb, small town, and farm, the largest percentage, 32 percent, chose a small town; another 23 percent chose the farm. *Sixty percent of the people in this study live where they do not want to, just to make money.* This is part of the decision to get out. To not *have* to live somewhere *just* to earn a living.

Intrinsic to the move is an idealistic longing for the land. Where do people go? To places glimpsed in childhood, where the smells of the sea or the pines or the thin mountain air act as Proust's *petite madeleine* on the bombarded city brain. Camp, college, trips with parents— places lived in dreams, which make you say, "Someday I want to come back here," even if you've only been there in your head.

In a house in a valley with trees all around, or in a cabin on a hill with valleys all around. On the baked but beautiful Southwestern sand or the rude and rocky New England coast—wherever people choose to get out to— the land is its own reason. Does it make any sense to ask why a couple would rather live in a two-hundred-year-old farmhouse on ten acres of meadow with its own fishy stream running through instead of in their loft on the Lower East Side over a pipe fitter's factory? There's even no wondering why a suburban home with Formica counters and a bathroom that works would be abandoned for an old hotel hugging a cove on the Atlantic shore. It's the urge to cultivate one's own garden, knowing that it's not important whether anything ever actually grows there.

The Gauguin Syndrome

I can just see me on a tropical island,
Riding the surf and drinking cocoanut wine,
Having me fun with golden girls in the sand,
Chasing the sun through an innocent land,
Leaving The Straight Life behind.*

Many of the people who leave ask themselves first,
"Where in the world would I most like to live?" Those
who have the easiest time of it can answer with a specific
address. Dreams can get you in trouble because they're
not so big on facts. One quick and common answer is a
desert isle, like Tahiti. When someone utters those three
syllables, you can tell it's the Gauguin Myth they have in
mind. This almost century-old fabrication was successful
because it was what we wanted to believe; one day M.
Paul Gauguin, uninspired stockbroker in Paris, woke up
and declared, "What I really want to do is go to a tropical island and become a painter." So he immediately
took off for Tahiti, where he lay under a palm tree and
alternately stroked and painted breasts, finding fulfillment in the primitive life and becoming rich and famous.
As Wayne Anderson's recent book *Gauguin's Paradise Lost*
points out, however, Gauguin was quite an accomplished, even mystical painter before he left France. He
was fleeing a Danish wife, to a rather Europeanized Pa-
peete and was always horrified and apart from the native
life. Instead of new inspiration for his art (which he got

---

* "The Straight Life," Sonny Curtis, © 1968 Viva Music, Inc. All rights reserved. Used by permission of Warner Bros. Music.

along with select island diseases), he was trying to recapture an early life with his mother in Peru.

But Gauguin and Tahiti still connote a possible dream, even though that island has become increasingly hostile toward Americans on vacation, not to mention permanent residence. It is almost impossible to get a visa to live there.

Islands figure high in the places we dream of. Finding a dream island is part of our romantic heritage. Robinson Crusoe spent twenty-four years on one. Mary Martin fell in love with Ezio Pinza on one, and in cartoons, neurotic men are always coming face to face with sexual fantasies on one. Real estate brokers make a brisk profit from the picking up and dropping of the United States' 26,325 pieces of land of ten acres or more that are entirely surrounded by water.

Besides Tahiti, the other island in the sun with the grand old reputation for getting out to is St. Thomas in the U.S. Virgin Islands. St. Thomas keeps reminding you it's an island as its inlets and outlets collide with little green foothills wading in the Caribbean. The streets are so lush with flowering trees you often find yourself walking on blossoms. An acre of land bought in 1939 for eleven dollars is now worth thirty or forty thousand.

St. Thomas was the dream island in 1949. For a generation of servicemen who were born too early to see the world on hundred-dollar student flights or international exchange programs, the Navy showed them the sweet side of the Caribbean. For many of the boys, in World War II, the high-contrast impression that St. Thomas sun made on their brains was a picture they carried back from the war. They couldn't get it out of their minds; it was too bright, too compelling. Thus, many of the current generation of successful St. Thomians are the ex-servicemen of World War II. They called themselves the 49ers, though they came all through the fifties and are coming still today.

The ways they made money were inspired only because they did not previously exist on the island; they were Promethean purveyors of dry cleaning, automobiles, construction. No one did what he was trained to do. It's said that brain surgeons clerked in men's stores; hairdressers sold real estate.

Nils Kurst, part of a new wave that arrived in the sixties, is an engineer who designed the Danish pavilion at the World's Fair in 1964. Not long after the fair closed, he left his hectic New York consulting business and a home in Greenwich, Connecticut, and moved to St. Thomas. Today he has diverse interests in building supplies, plumbing and electrical hardware, stationery supply, a restaurant, and a department store. In an accurate analysis of business on the island, he says, "I like to increase business only when there's some fun involved. Running around is not only satisfying—it's profitable. We suffer from recessions. But when building goes down, we have the stationery and the department store because cups and saucers always sell. It's like Coney Island. What you lose on the carrousel, you take home on the roller coaster."

The new proprietor of Budget Rent-A-Car, Alan Avdoyan, had a childhood daydream to live on an island. He says, "Your IQ goes up eighty points as soon as you get here. People who give up on this island are missing a great opportunity. It's like the English shoe salesman in Africa. He sees that nobody is wearing shoes so he goes back home. But the American shoe salesman says, 'Hey, nobody's wearing shoes. What an opportunity!' " Since his arrival in 1969, Alan has increased the Budget business over 300 percent. "When we got here we had 30 cars and only one ran. Now we have about 125."

This kind of get-up-and-go business talk doesn't sound like the quiet, simple life. But some of it is self-defense. Roger Moran left a large brick house in a Chicago suburb in the 1950s for a two-room apartment on St. Thomas with a stove that defrosted the refrigerator every time it was turned on. He also gave up advertising for real estate and is now one of the biggest brokers on the island. He says, "This is a free port. In a gin and tonic, the cheapest thing is the gin, then the ice, then the tonic. People work for need more than money. Nobody retires here. If you do, you start drinking for breakfast. You can commit suicide with a martini glass in eighteen months, if you don't have anything to do. That's all it takes. It's been done. People think they can come down here and just lie in the sun every day. You can get too much sun just walking from one place to another. You won't get sunburn, you'll get skin cancer."

So this incredibly beautiful island paradise lives in fear of demon gin and indolence. The alternative—to work hard, to become powerful and maybe even rich. Don Plantz, an ex-public relations man from Texas and a tough ex-Navy fighter pilot, says it: "It's the size of the puddle and the size of the frog." Along with an advertising agency and a postcard business, Plantz is the governor's press attaché. Plantz and his partner, Jacques

Ellison, who represented dairy interests in Madison, Connecticut, before coming to St. Thomas, helped elect the current governor, Melvin Evans, who was the first Negro ever elected in the obviously black Virgin Islands. Not only business power but political power is available to the Gotten Out.

The question arises, Are you leading an establishment life when you become the new establishment? For Ellison and Plantz, success is heady but inevitable. Says Plantz, "If something would happen at the other end of the button, you'd push it. Here, nothing happens so you forget about buttons. That's why people work harder here than they did at home, but it's for themselves." It's the same reason a man leaves a $12-million ad budget for a general store—it's all his own.

And the beauty. "It's so lush here," says one small businessman, "that every day you think it just can't last. I didn't think it would last every day for the last seven years and I'm sure it can't last the next seven."

"Out here you have to drink," says Plantz. "You have to cut that beauty with something."

What is it like now for a family getting out to St. Thomas? Opportunities exist, the sea is still soft and clear, but land costs are high. Roger Moran reports that a piece of acreage large enough to build a single-family residence was sold in 1957 for $3000, was then sold in 1960 for $9000, in 1961 for $12,500, and in 1972 for $34,500. "We have a form letter of discouragement for people who think they can come down here with an income of $500 a month or $5000 a year. There's not much they can do." Building costs are at about $35 a square foot (or the price of one maid per week). Costs Stateside range from $22 to $25 a square foot. The primary expense in any home building is a cistern. There is no fresh water supply on the island.

As two young women said, "It is the greatest test to see if you really want to come here—sell everything. We've had things, we've had antiques and silver. But you don't want things here. Besides, they get mildewed. You can't have crystal goblets because the maids break them. But you *can* have maids."

Still, St. Thomas is hardly thingless. Free port shops run over with Swiss watches and English woolens and more than all the liquor you can drink. Homes are far from shacks, set on slices into hills overlooking cerulean blue water. And though it's expensive, most of the Gotten Out live this way.

In 1965 Herman Wouk published *Don't Stop the Carnival*, a novel set in St. Thomas. He wrote:

> It is that, under all the parade of human effort and noise, today is like yesterday, and tomorrow will be like today . . . and that therefore the idea is to take things easy and enjoy the passing time under the sun.

The good life in St. Thomas is not as aimlessly and relentlessly hedonistic as Wouk tells us. There is room for the young, there is a place for hard work. As with all semilegends, there's a saying about this island: "If you're strong, you get stronger; if you're weak, you get weaker."

St. Thomas is the most settled island in the Caribbean and is probably a model for what the other islands will become. Dick Erb is manager of Caneel Bay on nearby

St. John's, one of the POSHest resorts in the world. Erb describes the state of the less civilized islands: "Paradise doesn't come easy. It takes all day just to survive. We take care of our own work. But there are no jobs here on the island. We get letters from lawyers making $40,000 a year wanting to run the campgrounds. A lot of hippies think they can live on cocoanuts and sleep on the ground. They find out soon that they can't." Not only do you have to work for paradise, you have to pay.

Dream Boats

Going down to the sea in ships (and never coming back) is the dream of many Sunday sailors. Sloan Wilson, in *Away from It All*, sets up the impracticality:

About two years ago I decided to buy a boat and run away to sea. In many ways it appeared to be a ridiculous decision. I was not a young man, foot-loose and fancy-free. On the contrary, I was forty-six years old, had two daughters in college, a son in his last year of preparatory school, and a two-year-old daughter who was not only the apple of my eye but a whole beribboned basket of fruit. I also had a young wife who was intrepid on Broadway but who had never been to sea in anything smaller than a Cunard liner and who professed a great fear of thunder and rain, never mind real storms. To compound the difficulties, I had failed to save much money and could not even dream of retiring aboard a yacht, however small.

Getting out to sea is only temporary unless you can find some way of getting bread from those waters. When Robert Manry first set lonesome foot on the *Tinkerbelle*, the thirty-foot boat he rebuilt himself, he was only on leave from the copy desk at *The Cleveland Plain Dealer*. After his seventy-eight-day solo voyage in the smallest craft ever to cross the Atlantic and the resulting hero's welcome in Falmouth, England, he never went back to his newspaper. He wrote a successful book, *Tinkerbelle*, and managed, through speeches and royalties, to live off his dream boat for six years until his death in 1971.

Most sea trips are briefer. A young St. Paul business-man recently sold all his suburban trappings—house, sta-tion wagon, camper—and put all the capital into a forty-foot yacht. With his wife and two small children he set out for the South Pacific. "We have enough money for two years at most, but I think that's all we need to clear our heads. Right now I can't even think of what I want to do when I get back because I don't know who I'll be then." Early last year, a forty-seven-year-old dentist named John Thompson from Birmingham, Michigan, decided to sell everything and sink (an unfortunate word) his money into a converted ocean freighter. The Thomp-sons loaded household goods, a piano, a Mustang, and a Rolls Royce into an aging 110-foot Dutch freighter he had bought for about $35,000. They were hoping to make an around-the-world cruise that would bring them back to Michigan in a year, to reassess their lives. But Thompson, the dentist, had the troubles of Odysseus, the soldier-king—and then some. They never got farther than a rather unworldly Miami, where they faced months of delay and thousands of dollars in repairs to their shattered vessel.

"You've got to figure it out. You've got to know what you're doing," says Bill Heuermann, a former investment counselor from San Francisco, who with his wife, Ea, and her three children skippers the fifty-eight-foot ketch *Jupiter* as a charter boat out of Yacht Haven Marina in St. Thomas. The Heuermanns are tanned and spirited and in their thirties. They left a huge Menlo Park house and swimming pool two years ago, to the horror of the wives and the glassy-eyed envy of the husbands in the neighborhood.

"Your dream changes," Bill warns. "Your initial concept may be escapist, but you have to be far more practical than that. Pure escapists cannot survive in a chartering environment. There is no such thing as coming to the Caribbean and living off the land. If there are fewer social pressures, there are more economic pressures.

"Many people think they can just hop on their thirty-five-foot cabin cruiser or sailing boat and make a living in the Caribbean. Even forty feet is too small. There is tremendous competition for charters. The ideal boat is fifty to sixty feet long, with adequate creature comforts."

It took Bill and Ea two years of travel and research to find the right boat in St. Thomas, and another few months to get it ready. "The first two months on the boat were the hardest. You have to adjust to not having any space. It was very hot and we had work to do," says Ea. "I couldn't get used to not having a telephone. If I heard a phone ring on television, I went to answer it."

The economics are not so escapist either. Bill says, "Boat costs range from $30,000 to $150,000. The average is about $60,000. You have to figure insurance as 5 percent of the current value of the boat, or $5000 on $100,000. You usually get $2000 deductible liability which protects you against wholesale damage. Then you have to figure annual maintenance between 10 percent and 30 percent of the boat value. That's what really gets you, the costs of repairs and replacements. Our initial outlays were much higher—we needed a new generator, which costs about $2500."

Bob Smith, manager of Ocean Enterprises, the charter-yacht association on St. Thomas, and himself a refugee from a Rhode Island lumber business, says, "In the season, you need to charter twelve weeks to survive, fifteen weeks to be comfortable, and twenty weeks to make money, assuming the boat is paid for free and clear. Twenty weeks means about $30,000 if you can do a lot of your own maintenance."

Bill and Ea charter for most of the winter season, which runs from November through April, but that still leaves them at least thirty weeks of their own, including time for repairs. But also time to read and take their own trips. I wondered if it was difficult having strangers aboard for a week, people you have to entertain and wait on. They said, "Most people are so anxious to have a good time, they're good sports. After the first day of getting their sea legs, they're eager to learn how to run the boat." Ea remembers one trip that did get sticky where each day she would silently hold up to Bill the number of fingers representing days left to spend with those people. "Worse come to worst," they always figure, "it's only a week."

They take a freezerful of food that Ea prepares for the

group. Sometimes there's a crew boy to do dishes, but not always. Ea says, "Food is a big problem. Fruits and vegetables have to be flown in from San Juan and Florida. But we have this thing about waking up at 3 A.M. and taunting each other—'Wouldn't you just love a nice cold peach? A pear?' What we get here are little fruits wrapped like a treasure at eighty-five cents apiece."

Despite fruit, the Heuermanns manage with apparent ease, doing what they want to do, together.

Dream Places

Americans who choose to live in Europe have not necessarily gotten out. More likely they have drifted out, inherited out, married out, been transferred out, and otherwise not consciously chosen an alternate way of life. John Bainbridge depicts these variations in a book of interviews with Americans in Europe called *Another Way of Living*. I don't consider any of his expatriates typical of the movement to a simpler life. Most of his subjects escaped to Europe for the reasons that most Americans have: the anonymity of their background and the uniqueness of being the only American around. This can result in a degree of status and social achievement that would have been impossible back home.

A typical expatriate says, "I'm terribly pleased to be invited by the Duchess of Rutland to her pony farm in Gloucestershire. If I had remained in Reading, Pa., I don't think the Duchess of Rutland would have invited me to her function." This man is in search of the lost society, seeking a European social structure, which for him is important to "transcend social barriers that I couldn't transcend in America."

A London art dealer, born in Brooklyn, says, "While I could have survived in New York, I don't know whether I could have gone . . . whether there are too many people like me there. England is a country, too, being a class society—and very much a class society—into which I was *rather* accepted, if I may use the euphemism, as somewhat of a gentleman. That gave me a kind of inner strength and security that I didn't particularly have in New York."

This searching after living well, which doesn't necessarily mean better, is evident among many Americans in Europe who are not there to study or to represent some American business. An American in Madrid says, "I have found that where my salary in the U.S. was about equivalent on the social-economic scale to that of an apprentice bricklayer, over here I can live as economic royalty on the same amount of money."

European cities, always nice places to visit, are not exactly free from the urban problems of U.S. cities. To go there usually is a trade-off, not a move out. As for making it in the provinces in a small business, the odds of acceptance, of language, of making money, of income tax are just a lot better in Vermont than in the Vosges. One couple I interviewed, Don and Lila Madtson, gave up a thriving family jewelry business in Kansas and went to Palma, Majorca, with thoughts of settling. Disillusioned, they chose Santa Fe, New Mexico, instead: "In Europe you're always having to defend or explain American political actions. You are always The American and as such are spokesman for things you may not even understand or agree with. And if you don't like that position, you can forget about being an American and try to assimilate, which is hard but okay if you never want to come back. We could never forget that we were Americans, and not through any special love of country, but out of honestly seeing what we are, we compromised and found our Spain in the Southwest."

In 1968–69, 3448 Americans emigrated to Australia. In 1970–71, the number jumped to 5500. In 1971–72, there were even more, 6330. The Gallup poll based on a survey in 1971 shows that close to 8 million Americans would pack off to Australia if they were "free to do so." The discontent that causes 8 million people to want to leave this country is not hard to understand. The myth that draws them to Australia is a little more complicated.

The impressive size of the continent is a lure in itself. With a population of only 12 million, Australia is like spreading the population of Pennsylvania throughout the continental United States. The myth of the Wild West, of the pioneer, is one of the sustaining notions of American life. And many Americans see in Australia a chance to relive covered-wagon days in their own lifetime. It's the immortalized Australian Outback—inhabited mainly by sheep and kangaroos and wombats, emus, platypuses, and dugongs. Golden opportunity, except for one thing—water. The Outback, fully three-quarters of the continent, is an arid plateau, suitable for grazing, but not for cropping. (As for the cowboy lore, one American living in Australia says, "Australians can't understand that Americans treasure their right to bear arms and often settle their disputes with guns," shooting down the shoot-'em-up image.) In reality, most of Australia's 12 million people live in the narrow strip between the coastal mountains and the shore, with the densest population centered around the cities, from Brisbane to Sydney, Canberra, and Melbourne. This bit of geography to erase for good the aura of wide-open spaces, unless you're into livestock.

Another thing Americans learn later than sooner about Australia is that they'll probably be living in a city or a suburb—which is where the jobs are—and the salary level is at least one-third lower than American scale. A sampling of government figures indicates that teachers earn between $3500 and $7000; middle management in business pays about $6000 to $9000. Senior engineers, foresters, dentists could aspire to a $10,000 income. Income tax is far steeper than in the United States; however, a rather comprehensive national medical program is paid for by taxes rather than private bills. Although salaries are lower, the cost of living is not. Rent, food, and clothing are comparable to the United States. Electrical appliances cost quite a bit more.

What, then, is so great about Australia? "The pace," Americans answer. "You don't feel as if you have to keep up with the Joneses." "Australians value their leisure and sports and don't care about work as much as Americans do." There are few shops or businesses open after Saturday noon or after 5 P.M. "It's like growing up in the States in the fifties," one young couple said. Some enterprising people turn the clock back further than that. Fifty, sixty years, maybe, and see the mining and business potential equal to the States at the turn of the century.

A land of business opportunity is not all evil, of course, unless we see it throwing itself into the same abyss of bureaucracy, corporate anonymity, and technological omnipotence that made us want to get out to begin with. There are signs of this. Australia has in the past pursued a very tight immigration policy where it, in effect, imports the jobs, not the man. According to Lionel Mead, chief immigration attaché to the Australian embassy in Washington, a young, professional family man who already has a job lined up in Australia would be high on the preferred list and even qualify for "assisted passage," where the Australian government pays up to three hundred dollars on each adult plane ticket and a percentage of a child's, providing the family stays for two years. The statistics say that if you stay for two years you're theirs.

Mead says the Australians are especially interested in people with degrees and experience in any kind of engineering, accounting, geology, and the biological sciences. His attitude is rather skeptical toward those professionals who do not want to take jobs in their fields and want to get out and live a different way of life. "Australia tries to discourage the El Dorado image in potential immigrants," Mead says. So, if you are an engineer, they want you as an engineer, not as a shopkeeper or a small farmer, for which you have no experience. "We would tend to deny permanent visas to Americans without sufficient funds or job plans." To start even a small farm in Australia, Mead estimates, would cost well into the $50,000s.

Two American couples who came to Australia and stayed have written a frank little book called *Australia,*

What's It Really Like? (You can get a copy by writing Southern Cross Publications, P.O. Box 99, Orlando, Florida 32802.) It's a paperback full of pros and cons and local newspaper advertisements for food, housing, clothing, appliances. According to the book, you'll "like the way Australians like Americans" and "you'll be surprised to find the Government's bureaucracy is worse than America's." You won't mind driving on the left, they say, but "it will worry you that Australia has one of the worst highway safety records in the world. You won't lack for entertainment" but "you won't like the housing that's available nor the price you have to pay for a flat (apartment)." Australia gets mixed reviews, at best.

A particularly moving tape from an American family who migrated to Australia, however, documents another function that continent has for Americans who want to get out. It is the New World as our country once was—a refuge for political dissenters. Dr. Dugald McClean and his wife, Carolyn, are native Nebraskans. Although Dr. McClean still works in psychiatry and hasn't changed his life-style in the professional sense, his income has dropped 50 percent, and as Carolyn says, they live well without dishwasher or disposal, clothes washer or second car.

After Dr. McClean's medical education in Omaha, he was "conscripted," as he says, as a doctor in the Army Medical Corps. His supposed two-year service tour was extended another two and a half years by the Korean War. He was stationed in Hawaii, where as a member of the surgical services he saw "tens of thousands of soldiers, victims of the Korean tragedy, pass through Honolulu." Once out of the army and as a result of the horror of war

they felt, the McCleans became interested in the United
Nations. They became members of the Society of Friends
(Quakers). Then back to a residency in psychiatry in
Lincoln, Nebraska.

Dr. McClean continues, "We had become pacifists by
that time, and the total national purpose of the United
States from our pacifist position seemed almost intolerable in that the great amount of money and human investment was in the destructive forces of the cold war. In Lincoln and Omaha were strong concentrations of the
Strategic Air Command. I've always said we were in Nebraska before the missiles came, and it wasn't big enough
for both of us. That's a glib explanation, but we lived
through the Berlin crisis and the Cuban crisis and we had
two sons coming up for the draft and we felt we could no
longer support the national purpose of the U.S.

"One of the most discouraging things at that time, remember this was 1956 to 1963, was the apathy of all age
groups. We were active in the United Nations and also
almost charter members, at least in the Midwest, of Sane
Nuclear Policy, and we seemed like a minute group of
people that were concerned about these issues at that
time. Had we been living in the U.S. at a later date, or
come to our position later, we may not have left, because
of the involvement that many people demonstrated in the
later sixties.

"But from our point of view in 1961–62, rather than be
entirely negative and demonstrate against things at that
time, we wanted to seek another place to live where we
could express our concerns more positively. We looked at
New Zealand, Tasmania, Costa Rica, and New South

Wales, Australia, and of them all, New South Wales seemed most eager for us to come."

The McCleans and their four children now feel in the bustling city of Sydney more control over their political destiny than in the United States, where the "masses of society seemed to be steamrolling over the issues we wish to further." Still members of the Society of Friends, as well as of the Australian peace movement and ecology action groups, the McCleans feel able to make positive progress, to affect their destiny. "In Australia it is smaller and you can personally know members of Parliament and leaders in various fields. We are concerned with more local, less national issues, but they are a size we can handle."

If I sound rather negative about leaving this country, it's because I have prejudices of my own. When you live abroad, you always feel like you can go home if things get rough, and that's a pull that exerts itself almost unconsciously. It is a cushion that can weaken your independence. Getting out is, after all, the move of a lifetime. It's hard enough changing a whole life pattern without complications of language and money and strangeness to deal with. Arbitrary? Maybe. It seems to me, however, that to go to live in another country, whether it is New Zealand, Israel, or even Canada, is a different experience. Complicating, perhaps, rather than simplifying. It is looking for an exotic framework for the same old problems rather than coming to terms with, and maybe even eliminating, them.

6

See America First

Dear Sir:

We are a younger couple looking for a place where a family can enjoy a serene quality of life, where surroundings and climate are beautiful. We realize that honest effort is required to establish ourselves and we are willing to put forth that effort. From magazine articles and a visit, we have noticed northern New Mexico as an area where civilized values and respect for the environment aren't overwhelmed by the urban rat race. This region seems to be an ideal place for our family to establish a home and contribute our talents.

From a letter to the New Mexico
Department of Development, 1970

The traditional pattern of population movement to the cities has given us a stereotype about the rest of the country it doesn't deserve. Because all the bright young people left the small towns for the big city, the sticks by definition have become the direct opposite of where-it's-at-ness. From the headquarters of television networks to the top of the Time-Life Building, the Mediamakers (themselves in from the country) reinforce these stereotypes. No one in his right mind, for example, would intentionally go to West Virginia or Mississippi to live unless he were into a movement, like poverty or civil rights. Our news images give us preconceptions that rule out potentially viable places. These preconceived images get in the way of the reality of living in the exurbs far outside the large cities: availability of land, possibilities of starting small businesses, climate, and the chance to live somewhere where everybody doesn't talk the same, think the same, or dress the same.

In contemplating moving to the sticks, the worry should not be the fear of social contamination by boorish rurals. Much worse is the threat of invasion by shopping centers. In the late sixties, the most significant flow of people has not been from small towns to cities but from the cities to the suburbs, as fast as their station wagons could carry them. What used to be referred to as the ex-urbs—beyond the suburbs—has been gobbled up into the suburb proper (or improper). Which really means that in many of the good rural and small towns, they're tearing down the trees and paving grass with parking lots. The boundaries between town and country are blurred by economic expedience. Grotesque shopping malls, emporia of tack, with their accompanying string of fast-food franchises, are eating up this country. And vice versa.

In deciding where to get out to, it certainly is important to be a reasonable distance from the madding crowd. (Far but not too far, since you will probably need a market for whatever it is you'll do.) But realize that the city as an interchange of people and goods is not so pernicious as the satellite shopping centers that have nowhere to grow but out.

It is this monstrous growth without plan that has ruined the country's first and best places to get out to—California and Florida.

For the first time in California's history, as many people moved out in 1970 as moved in. California, in fact, has become one of the prime places to get out from. Since 1970, inquiries about living in New Mexico from Californians far outnumbered inquiries from those in states like Pennsylvania, Michigan, or Ohio. Although there have been rumblings in the Florida State Senate restricting (or not encouraging) growth, the Miami Beach Mentality is far too prevalent and powerful to stand for cutting back. And because many folks go to Florida for the rest of their days, fewer want to leave.

Arizona was another place in the sun, now glutted with the garbage of growth to the point where many of the staunchest devotees of Phoenix and Scottsdale are looking for greener and certainly cleaner valleys. Colorado, too, suffers from a come-hither image that just brought too many people. Those who successfully got out to Colorado did so in the past ten years, rather than the past two. The men who built Aspen started even earlier than that. Many were members of the Tenth Mountain Division in World War II, which fought around Livorno in the Apennines. They loved the old mom and pop lodges, snow, and skiing. And after the war they didn't go back to Jersey City. Like their counterparts who got out to St. Thomas, these men also got out; they built Aspen and Vail and Colorado Springs as ski centers. They also got into the businesses of manufacturing and selling ski equipment and clothing. But that was twenty years ago and Aspen is now big business, divided by those who want it to grow and those who don't—a familiar tug of war. Some of the Colorado originals have moved on to whiter pastures like Jackson Hole, Wyoming. To begin it all again? Colorado is still a good place to go. But it has been discovered, which means you have to pay. It also means that a social climate exists there that sustains small business and emphasizes outdoor life. It is perfectly suited to a city refugee who doesn't want to forsake society.

Vermont shares Colorado's popularity, without its industry or its size. At this writing, Vermont probably has replaced Colorado as *the* most popular place to get out to. Less than half the land in the state is owned by natives. In 1968, a Department of Development survey showed more than 22,000 vacation houses, more than half owned by out-of-staters. But that's a misleading figure, for in the last five years Vermont has experienced its largest growth rate. Nobody's counting, but since 1968 the number has probably quadrupled. As close as the Planning Department can estimate, between 10 and 20 percent of those have become permanent residences. Meaningless figures until you get specific.

Alasdair Munro was a vice-president of McCann-Erickson, responsible for the Coca-Cola account, among others. He had one of the thousands of vacation houses, and for years, Munro and his family would spend winter weekends in Vermont. In the past few years, however, they began to spend summers there too, Munro commuting by jet from New York on weekends. Soon the Munros realized that they had hardly a life at all back in Darien, where they really lived. In 1970–71 Munro, forty-three, began asking, "Why should I have to wait till I'm sixty-five to live the way I want to?" So he got out of McCann,

and by selling his company's stock, bought into a real estate business in the Sugarbush Valley. In the town of
Waitsfield, Munro works a lot harder than one would expect with all that skiing around. (He estimated that during his first year in Vermont, he skied only five days,
compared to about thirty when he was still commuting.)
Munro says of the Vermont boom, "I get about a half
dozen people in my office every week who want to get out
of New York or Boston. They just don't know what they
can do here to make a living. Two disillusioned lawyers I
know are banging nails on a construction job, which is
the only work they can find. I could sell every Christmas
tree farm or maple sugar bush I could get my hands on—
they're the viable businesses everyone wants. But there
aren't many for sale. There also aren't many little old
farmhouses with charm and several acres left either. And
when they come up for sale, they're $50,000 and $60,000
instead of the $25,000 they used to be."

Some areas of Vermont have already gone out of
control. Munro calls Stowe "a white-on-white Coney
Island." And indeed while the state has finally been able
this year to control roadside signs and billboarding with a
handsome standard signboard in sans-serif type, there is
no one to stop those ersatz chalets in the prevalent Early
Cuckoo Clock style. There are over eight hundred vacation houses admittedly well-nestled in the relatively small
Sugarbush Valley alone, more than half built in the last
five years. This is not all good.

Progress, of course, spawns business, which in turn
brings people. Route 100, which crosses the southern part
of the state, is given over to the tourists. Shoppers, weekend leaf watchers, and snow watchers drive five hours

into the country, not to walk on woodsy paths but to shop. And they go home, the tourist shoppers, with their little boxes of maple-sugar candy in the shape of leaves, their made-yesterday olde New England cooking utensils, and maybe a gallon of cider bottled in plastic. Tourists become fatigued with the traffic on two-lane roads, hassled by having to trek the family through quaint olde stores with midget doorways and slanted floors, anxious over the decision of which wood-framed reproduction of an autumn hillside they never saw would go best in their living room.

It's that paradox again. Getting out to the great land inevitably means business from tourism in a small shop or a restaurant or an inn. But that business will be supported by the number of people flocking to the state. It's for you to decide how many people is too many. You can still find a lot of very sleepy little places in Vermont. In Connecticut, even. And western Massachusetts.

New England in the seventies finds itself in a strange economic situation. Much of the industry long ago took its business to Dixie, leaving textile mills and factories to stand empty in the crossroads of many towns. You can see the late afternoon sun filter through one side of the building and out the other, unimpeded by the dark forms of machinery or the moving shadows of men at work. On the Maine coast, sardine canneries stand open and empty, victims of the whims of American appetite. Jobs are scarce. And with the burgeoning tourist business, so is land. It is far more expensive than the impoverished look of many towns would suggest. Real estate developers went on a picnic in New England about five years ago and they never left. But even the baroque imagination of real estate excess is limited in New England. There may be thousands of costly pseudo-Alpine A-frames, but there will never be high rises in the White Mountains.

Nor will there be high rises in Santa Fe, New Mexico. New Mexico gets almost two thousand letters a year not just requesting travel information but asking the big question—"How will it be for me and my family if we move here?" New Mexico is just moving out of a sociohistorical period when it saw the frantic coming and gradual dissolution of communal living. The most famous communes were New Buffalo and the Hog Farm. Kids were drawn to the Indian country. In New Mexico, land was cheap and they could ally themselves with the life cycles of Indians and of the earth. Only they didn't realize it gets cold in the winter. Really cold, with snow. And they hadn't planned on food for the time it took a cycle of crops to grow. The kids learned quickly that they couldn't make it off the arid land in New Mexico, where about sixty acres of grazing land is needed per head of cattle. Those who have stayed are into an artisan culture that finds its greatest expression in Santa Fe, one of the most unique cities left in this country.

Santa Fe has just enough business and more than enough artistic spirit to encourage and patronize people who will earnestly go into little business—pottery, leathercraft, glassblowing. The life in Santa Fe is an excellent combination of tourists/buyers in the summer and long quiet winters to work through. Its dusty streets and walled-in adobes hide away a number of different ways of living. And though it is said of Santa Fe, as of most small towns, that you can sneeze on one side of town and someone will say "God bless you" on the other, no one is about to question your right to sneeze. Although Santa Fe is the seat of state government, the university, and the opera, it is less pretentious than the much-touted art colony of Taos. Taos is artsy like Greenwich Village or Chicago's Old Town, purely commercial. On the facades of its shops, huge Master Charge and BankAmericard signs hang outside like medieval flags—pop-art commerce. Taos is steeped in the kitsch of the Southwest, which is even more of an exploitation of Indians than building cement-block ranch houses in front of their hogons. It may be overreaction, but Taos even makes the local Kentucky Fried Chicken look straight because it at least has the integrity to be what it seems.

Taos is the exception, however. Like Albuquerque it has succumbed to the modern world. But there are many villages, like Truchas, for instance, whose little painted houses hug the road so close you can reach out and touch the plastic flowers in their windows. There is the air of a different culture, one-third Mexican, one-third Spanish-American, one-third Anglo, in most small New Mexican towns. On some of the hilly back roads, a donkey is seen more frequently than a car; if you do see a car, it's usually some broken-down twenty-year-old Buick in pieces in the front yard.

Transplanted outsiders like to talk about the natural rhythm of New Mexico: mañana is good enough. Not as slow as Mexico, but slow. The light, they say, is rich and rare, changing every time you look out a window. There

is land available around Santa Fe, but moving out of
town means putting in your own water and electricity.
The old adobes, wonderful spaces with courtyards and
cavelike fireplaces, have been seen in just enough slick
shelter magazines to be substantially overpriced.

The state travel director of Utah is said to have re-
marked, "Our greatest product is egress." In that line of
business, Utah is joined by neighboring Wyoming, Montana, and Idaho, which all have very good state universi-
ties but not enough real business to keep the talent at
home. These Western states face the same dilemma states
like Maine do: there is a desperate need for big industry
to supply jobs. This conflicts with a superstrong desire
to preserve the environment. Frank Norris, Wyoming's
bright-eyed, easy-talking tourist director, says, "The
fiercest ecologists are people who moved here in the last
six months. They figure, 'We're here, now lock the
door!' " As for small businesses starting up, it's a long
way between towns, and longer between people. Small
ranchers are selling out like the small farmer in the Midwest. "It's possible," Norris says, "to grub it out on a
small ranch. But the cattleman image is not as strong as
it used to be. In Wyoming, we raise cattle for dignity and
sheep for money."

Tourism is second to agriculture in Wyoming's economy. And while tourism often has the ring of exploitation
about it, it is a very good way to live on the land you love
and make money too. Jackson, Wyoming, the town nearest to Jackson Hole, the resort, has a river running
through it you can drink from. In 1970 there were five

tourist-oriented businesses. The number jumped to forty in 1971. Jackson, like Cody and Cheyenne, has a lot of hand-hewn hokiness about it. It looks like every Western movie in the world was made there, but somehow you don't mind.

Today there is a great buying up of land in the West. It's a movement that recognizes all the ballyhoo of the last frontier as gospel. This is not, of course, the only land left to uncivilized man, as Chet Huntley would have us believe. (Huntley raced out into the setting sun of Montana from NBC's bright lights only to grab the spotlight again to plug Big Sky Country and his development investments.) Towns like Billings and Bozeman, Montana, are filling up with the Gotten Out, many of whom will take any kind of work just to live there.

While all the Rocky Mountain states except Colorado are receptive and helpful to a prospective resident, don't expect the same attitude in Oregon, which has absorbed much of California's overflow. Its attitude is said to be one of "come and visit us again and again. But for heaven's sake, don't come here to live." Oregon fears a rise in the unemployment rate because of jobless and disillusioned Californians and dreads the encroachment of industry in a primarily agricultural state.

But urban refugees shun industry almost as much as Oregon does, and that means an ever-increasing search for rural places to get out to. We have to change our images of places if we are looking for land for a garden, open fields to pick wild flowers, woods to gather holly and to shoot down mistletoe from the top of an oak. I'm talking about the changes that are happening in places like West Virginia.

An entire colony of former antipoverty workers in VISTA has chosen to come back to live in Appalachia. As one welfare worker from Brooklyn says, "I get a lot of pleasure in living on the land. I get an ecstatic joy out of seeing things grow. Like a little boy, I run in and tell my wife when I see something coming up. It's a real comfort."

Says another rural activist, "You want to put on bib overalls, take off your shoes, walk up and down the hollow and sit on people's porches and talk."

A little piece in the *Media Industry Newsletter* in its mergers and acquisitions column indicates the kind of change taking place:

> Robert Arnold, former senior vp of First National City Bank of New York, and Stan Meseroll, previously managing editor of *Sports Afield* magazine, acquired *Glenville Democrat* and *Glenville Pathfinder*, combined circulation 3,300, two weekly newspapers in Gilmer County, West Va. Includes the building and equipment from Linn B. Hickman. Terms: $43,000.

A little digging showed that Meseroll first went to West Virginia on a hunting trip with the state's tourism director and was so enchanted with the country life that he went back to his magazine and decided he wanted to live what he had only been publishing. He talked his good friend, Robert Arnold, into the weekly newspaper business, called his friend the tourism director, and said, "Guess what. I'm coming down there."

It has always seemed strange to me that more people don't get out to the hills of north Georgia, the mountains of western North Carolina, or the rolling pinelands of Mississippi. The obvious answer, of course, is the race situation. Urban dwellers, feeling locked in by fear of violence, want to get away as far as possible. Some places cater to that fear. A brochure about southern Missouri called *Land in the Ozarks* boasts, "Race problems? We don't have 'em. No Negroes in Dallas County."

No one I have interviewed has mentioned the race struggle as a reason to leave riot-prone inner cities or besieged white suburbs (it's quite unfashionable to mention it), but articles discussing the fears of the American people cite racial militance and violence as prime reasons to get out. I think the insular quality of our information sources tends to downplay all but the most proximate race struggle. People who move in fear make a great mistake. The race struggle goes on in every hamlet in the world where more than one kind of people live together. Minorities worldwide are beginning to have their say, even if it is only a local scream. New Mexicans, for instance, are involved in the plight of increasingly militant Chicanos, even if the rest of the world isn't. One hundred thirty thousand aborigines in Australia are demanding their rights at long last, even if we don't know about it. Native islanders in the Caribbean have organized their resentment against white exploiters. The struggle is worldwide and as serious in south Philadelphia as it is in Lander, Wyoming, where Rotarian ladies give parties and fur coats to middle-class Japanese exchange students and totally ignore an entire reservation of Shoshoni Indians that don't have enough status as a cause for them.

The machinery of protest is available to minorities everywhere. And if the South was once a place to be feared by do-gooder white liberals, it is probably, today, and especially on the rural level, one of the few places where blacks and whites *can* exist together.

A Tale of Two Towns

There are two kinds of towns to retreat to. One is the movie-lot version of small-town America, whose streets are wide enough for parades and are named for prominent local citizens or trees. In this kind of town, A-town, there's a way of doing things based on the way it's always been done. Second and third generations are still in evidence, their identities tied to street addresses that mean something only at home. A-town has a Welcome Wagonful of community spirit. The lyings down and the risings up of its citizens comprise a lending library of open books.

B-town is a collection of people who just happen to be living near each other. They are too different to share a common identity and too independent to need one. They have a hard time agreeing on schools of politics, so diffuse are their interests. B-town lives and lets live without too many moral or social judgments. More liberal but less friendly.

In typing a town you have to look carefully and not be prejudiced by location. Places change. A-town, a small Midwestern farming community, whose life once flowed around the courthouse square and the church, can evolve into B-town. It can happen when the old pillars of the community give out, or die off and are replaced by younger or different people who don't remember how it was way back when and don't particularly care. Charlotte Amalie on St. Thomas was originally a B-haven of natives and assorted castaways from the American scene. And although there's plenty of room for original lifestyles, the new establishment on St. Thomas has the institutions and the land pretty much in control, like a tight little A-town.

If small towns and rural areas are indeed going to be the alternative to the city/suburb, that alternative must be studied carefully. A family that needs the comfort of constant community will want to nestle into A-town. A more insular, self-contained family unit would opt for B-town.

York, Maine, is an A-town if there ever was one. Its venerable town buildings are painted lily white, diligently maintained by the townspeople, many of whom are descendants of the original settlers. The church with its bright white steeple shooting up into a Puritan blue sky has the date 1747 on its facade. Across the street from the church is an old gaol (jail)—circa 1658—painted in the rich maroon of Colonial America. The hill from the jail slopes down past the gallows on the front lawn quite conveniently into a cemetery, vast and green and laden with old stones—the proof of birthright. Even now a mother, her daughter, and her daughter's daughter are making rubbings from the grave stones, sitting there in the well-kept green grass in their Liberty print cotton dresses with McMullan collars.

Fred and Rosemarie Lesswing started coming to York and its neighboring coastal communities of York Harbor and York Beach for five years before they ever thought of getting out. Fred was an executive with General Electric and as the quintessential company man, had moved his family ten times in twelve years, always into GE communities in Syracuse, Darien, and Pittsfield. With each move came a promotion, with each promotion a new set of cost-improvement goals that had to be met. The Lesswings looked ahead to a company life that would become increasingly more inbred as the social and personal demands became greater with upper management. Although the progress and financial rewards were great, Fred says, "There was still the feeling at the end of each year that even though you were meeting your goals, they were just small figures in a great corporation. And after I'd done the job once, there was nothing to interest me in doing the same thing for another year. The constant moving was hard on our family [four children]. We didn't have any friends outside GE and certainly no permanent, root-type people. Our kids weren't able to keep friendships either, moving so much. GE was very good to us. But I wanted something with a lot more challenge. And we wanted roots."

After a few preliminary inquiries into real estate in the York area, the Lesswings had almost decided to buy a house on remote Deer Isle in Maine, to renovate it and sell it. Then they happened to see an ad in *Down East* magazine: N. G. Marshall Hardware in downtown York Village was for sale. They decided to buy it immediately, with money from the sale of their house, a little savings, and help from the Maine National Bank. They had to accept Nat Marshall's inventory estimate of $35,000. In forty-five years of business, Nat had never taken an inventory. When Fred finally did take stock six months later, he found that Marshall had been only $200 off.

Old Nat Marshall wasn't just a nuts-and-bolts man, but part of the revered Marshall family of York, owners of Marshall House, the hamlet's fine inn. Nat himself was an esteemed selectman and would open his store year round at 4 or 5 A.M., to be ready for the building contractors. The old families of York were wary of this youngster in to take over Nat's store. (Fred was thirty-nine.) He felt they were testing him for at least the first six months. "You have to get used to their way of doing business. I mean I was drilled for fifteen years in the company toward greater and greater efficiency. The first day I opened this store, five men came and sat down to talk and they stayed four hours. They're just not in a hurry, and that's a hard thing to learn. But I go out of my way to listen."

He talks about the A-town mentality. "There are a lot of old families in York. Mostly Protestant. Down Easters. I'm a Catholic and I feel they treat me without prejudice. But I do think they'd be critical of blacks if they were to come here to live. You can see it in their attitude towards black tourists who come through. These people have strong moral judgments. It's unbelievable how word gets around. People love to talk and gossip. There's nothing confidential. But then you know that before you come.

"The average guy is concerned about money. Their families were traders in early Maine days and they'll say 'that looks like a good trade' instead of price. I've learned you can't just have one price, you've got to bargain with them; they'll travel over fifteen miles to Portsmouth, New Hampshire, to get something ten cents cheaper. People warned me when I got into this store, 'Don't change anything.' But change is the excitement of this business. I know every result comes from what I do and I try many angles. First I bought the old post office next door and broke through the wall. Then I wanted to put board and batten on the facade. And some of the old ladies came in and said, 'What is the historical society going to say if you don't paint it white?' They gradually accepted the new facade, but you've got to go slow—soft-pedal things. You don't want to get the town fathers up in arms over a neon sign."

In the summer, the Yorks (Village, Beach, and Harbor) are crammed with twenty thousand vacationers, weekenders, and the summer people. In the winter, the population of the three towns shrinks to one-quarter that number. The winter nights are filled with volleyball games, old-fashioned rummage sales and skating parties, the Merrymakers Club and the Townspeople's Club. It's an easy-going group—several younger people have gone into business for themselves in York and the Lesswings feel they have the roots they're looking for. They found a big old red Victorian house facing the Atlantic, where, says Rosemarie, "Nobody locks doors. The philosophy is that if you have something worth stealing, you shouldn't have it. You see," she continues, "it's the kind of a town where if you wind up in the hospital, the butcher sends you flowers. If someone's house should catch on fire, know them or not, you rush over there with drop cloths. We always know when there's a fire. Our main store employee is a volunteer fireman, and when he hears the bells he runs out no matter what he's doing."

There's a motto tacked to the refrigerator in the Lesswings' kitchen. It says, "A gatherer is always followed by a scatterer." It means, they say, "that no matter how much you save up and hoard away, someone's going to come along and spend it after you. So, you cut your salary in half and are happier for it." Accordingly, all six Lesswings have bicycles, even though they're eating away the profits of the store. Fred's bike was taken from the store window, giving in to a beautiful summer Sunday. Now the six can be seen of a Sunday morning heading toward the beach on bicycles. "It's fun," says Fred. "People driving by wave in amusement. Besides, it's good advertising."

Cerrillos, New Mexico, is a B-town. Located over thirty miles southwest of Santa Fe, it was once a mining center with almost three thousand people in its boom days. It became shortly after that, for tourist purposes, a ghost town. Its saloons and little shops stood virtually empty for decades. But somehow the good places don't die, and Cerrillos has come quite alive again. Someone has bought the old saloon. Disenchanted kids, brought down by a bad experience at some commune, gather here not to do anything more than try to get it back together. In the general store, a good old boy sits in a tilted chair, his feet on a counter that displays new-age relics—whiskey bottles, empty, and a lot of buttons. The Spanish-American families who have been here all along chase their chickens around a fenced-in front yard of dirt. Or they sit on the flat front porches of their mud-brick adobe houses and watch little curls of dust being carried off toward the horizon.

The brown, arid, sandy soil, flat until it runs off into the mountains beyond, supports its own kind of growth: little tufts of buffalo grass that turn green just after a rain, then brown again; bear grass, a kind of spiky yucca; the blue gray chamisa bush; scrub cedar; and a little tree cactus called cholla.

There are now about fifty people in Cerrillos. Among the relative newcomers are Don and Barbara Wright and their children, who operate The Second Source, a jewelry and leather shop around the dusty corner from the main block.

The Wrights came from Pennsylvania. After Don had tired of advertising, they settled on the Altoona Campus of Penn State, where, for several years, he taught art and Barbara was an executive secretary for a company that made radio crystals. Don and the university differed, and the Wrights decided to get out. As fast as they could, they converted a school bus to a camper and left. Once they had decided to go and live "where we want to and not where a job puts you," they couldn't wait. They gave the house they were buying, a twenty-two-room mansion on four and one-half acres, back to the people they were buying it from. They said the hell with such things as equity and took off.

When they first got to Cerrillos, the Wrights rented two rooms with neither water nor heat for twenty dollars a month. Don started making silver jewelry, and when the landlord gave them fifty dollars to put heat in, Don used the money to hitchhike to San Francisco, where he sold the jewelry and made contacts. That was in July, 1968.

Now the Wrights are past the struggling point and have a good little shop at the front of their adobe house, a fairly complete gold-jewelry-making facility, and room for Barbara to sew leather.

But it's not all that simple. "We didn't come out here to do this work. We wanted to establish an economic base and have a house that no one could take away from us. But the problem point is when to stop. It's almost impossible to turn down business and just say I don't feel like working. It's hard to put limits on yourself."

Barbara explains: "We keep thinking that the good life is to work awhile at big motor things and the rest of the day to do small motor things."

Don: "But the business seems to have a life of its own."

Barbara: "I keep pressing to do less. I think it's slavery if you are so hung up in your business you can't stop. That's why we came here. To lead a less synthetic life. If you can walk rather than ride, grow your food and make your clothes rather than buy them, you become close to the basic life."

It is strange that in a town like Cerrillos, B-town, the Wrights have become community leaders of a sort. You have to understand that they are not exactly the establishment type. As Barbara says, "If you have an art background you are always a little bit on the fringes." Don wears one thin gold earring and has never voted in his life. Yet, as he says, "I tend to get involved. I tried to start a school here. I had the building and a teacher but I couldn't get the parents to agree to commit the money in

advance, so the whole thing fell through. Then we tried
to organize a food cooperative. Every family was going
into Santa Fe a couple of times a week and we could all
get together and buy in quantity and save time and
money. But the kids, the hippies if you want to call them
that, were against it. They said we were giving more
money to the establishment and associated us with the
straight society. It's funny. They'll come here and borrow
tools and break them or not bring them back, but when
we suggested this new co-op have a tool-lending place,
they wouldn't cooperate. They're so afraid of rules. These
kids dress like Indians and emulate the Indian life-style,
but when they refuse to work together, we say they just
aren't good Indians."

Don, who has never belonged to a civic association, did
succeed in getting a permanent water supply for the community. He created Los Cerrillos Mutual Domestic
Water Consumers' and Mutual Sewage Works Association, the irony he feels about it evident in the name.

"We're both very much growth people," they say. And
how do things grow in B-town? Read this from a recent
letter from the Wrights:

> We are opening a shop in Albuquerque in May.
> Went into partnership with a fellow who will han-
> dle the business. Our duty is to keep the shop
> stocked and to be in the shop on Saturdays to take
> orders. It will be a plush shop, only gold jewelry and
> a totally new line of leather. Our shop will continue
> here as long as necessary.
>
> And, we are endeavoring to purchase forty acres
> outside Cerrillos on the road to Santa Fe to build a

house, workshops, and, if necessary, a retail shop. But if the Albuquerque shop goes well, we may be able to get out of the shopkeeping business entirely. Hopefully these things will all mesh well together and one day in the not too distant future, we will have our economic and life core set up so that we need to produce less salable items and can give more time to self-sustenance.

7

Communes and Homesteading

Once you determine that working for someone else or the corporate system is not for you, you become faced with an almost terrible freedom. Options open up to you that you've never been able to consider before. Extreme ways of living may attract you.

But there are ways and there are ways. Total and monkish rejection of civilization and its jades is as unrealistic as blind perpetuation of it. Trying, as some defunct kid communes tried, to scratch a loaf of bread from arid, sandy soil is fake pioneering when there's pretty good bread in packages at the corner grocery.

We have become more infatuated with the wilderness

the farther we get from it. We feel it necessary to be able to survive in the most basic life conditions, mostly because we don't have to. Teaching survival techniques has become big business. Machismo camps like Outward Bound are flush with the rush of executives who pay several hundred dollars to be left in the woods for five days and exist on roots, only to return to their electric toothbrushes and Water Piks. Pioneers made do with what they had only until they could do better, which is how we got into this technocratic and very gross national product in the first place.

Equally misleading is the pastoral notion that the simple shepherd is living the only true and pure way of life. People who believe it have never truly smelled sheep. And never talked to the shepherd who'd probably give anything to get away.

People searching for what to get out to find themselves in a middle-class, middle-age dilemma where sudden, radical change to someone else's life-style comes off as a charade. Lost weekends in Essalen groups are as ludicrous as *Bob & Carol & Ted & Alice.* One hero of a *Wall Street Journal* series of articles called "The Great Escape: More Affluent Adults Quit Corporate World to Lead Simple Lives" shows how implausible getting cool can be. John Koehne is six feet six inches tall. His "faded red hair is tied in a ponytail and his moustache droops below the corners of his mouth. He wears a broad-brimmed leather hat, a heavy sheepskin coat, leather pants and high boots." Because of a weekend session at an encounter group, Koehne quit twenty years of work at the CIA, of all places, and with a camper decorated with peace symbols and a wife who was "reluctantly transformed," plans to leave his suburban Washington house with the yellow submarine painted on the side to start a commune of eight good friends based on "simplicity of life style and an end to materialism and status motivations." Good Luck. Experience has shown that communes are no place for refugees from the PTA, not to mention the CIA.

As Don and Barbara Wright, now of Cerrillos, New Mexico, found out in a crafts commune called Apache Creek in northern New Mexico. "We had only read about communal living but we felt it would work. We found out fast that we are not commune people. The way they had it set up, these people who had been in the rat race went the complete opposite direction—no rules. And you just can't get anything done without some kind of structure. Then we found out the leader was on some kind of fundamentalist religious trip. He insisted he had a direct pipeline to God, which we couldn't quite accept. So, even though we were beginning to build our own earth house, we left Apache Creek."

The counterculture can't just be put on with a new-old pair of blue jeans. The mentality that makes for successful communal living is not bred in suburbia, of upward striving and acquisition, of a fierce rigidity about sex and a fixation on money more powerful than that. So few middle-age, middle-class communes are successful because they can't make the leap from suburbia. Group consciousness? These people live the middle-class social plan where couples "socialize" but hardly ever touch, except in unruly drunkenness or adultery. Their sharing is limited to cups of sugar or maybe the second car. Most significant, their life thrust is wholly individual (in most families the work objective of the husband isn't even shared by the wife). Individuality is the opposite of community. To people who were raised in the system, being responsible to the common good of a group and to shared ideologies is nonfreedom. Unless you were the one who thought up the ideology first.

Dick Fairfield, editor and publisher of *The Modern Utopian*, a magazine devoted to the search for alternate lifestyles, has done the only thorough study of commune life that I trust. Because he sincerely believes there must be another way of living, he eagerly investigates each communal situation he visits. But he is too good a reporter not to admit where it doesn't work. His book *Communes, USA*, published by Penguin, is a thorough and straight study.

Fairfield reported on a group marriage experiment, Talsasen, which left the San Francisco Bay area for a commune in Oregon:

> They had carried on a brutal suburban existence—
> pharmacist and housewife, professor and housewife,
> etc. The men frustrated and the women unfulfilled.
> The country, the land, intimate friendships spelled
> liberation, freedom from the old unhappy pattern—
> they were desperate to start a newer and more
> fulfilling lifestyle. That desperation led them to
> move too quickly. Too many years of wrong habits
> could not be resolved so easily. Instead, seven des-
> perate people clung together, each shaking from the
> weight of his own lack of clarity. It was inevitable
> that that tiny group would be blown to bits.

I asked Dick whether he found many "ex-urban, rather establishment, corporate, involved types in communes." He said, "There are many of this type who do live in communes, often those types of communes which *minimize* the value of work. I went to Wheeler (Sheep Ridge) Ranch and Morning Star [both places, incidentally, where the traditional monogamous family and territorial imperative are exercised . . . where 'women retain their subordinate position . . . men roam the land in search of food,' both places, incidentally, now defunct] and found several who just went to dig the earth, nature, dope, subsistence living. There is often a strong reaction to work, and *especially organized* work, that is, work which is not completely self-motivated, among this type. Eventually, when this type of person finds what will motivate him, he'll work his tail off—building his own home, cultivating an organic garden, etc. Generally, however, this type tends to get into an individual pursuit that's more similar to where he came from—instead of producing for the boss/consumer, he produces directly to the consumer via handicrafts, small business, service."

For most people, it isn't enough to leave the system and go tune in on someone else's dream. If anyone's dream is involved, it's going to be his own. It seems that the only communal living situations that survive are those whose rules are spelled out much like a religion. In joining them, the will of the individual is subjugated to that of the group. Both work and play hours belong to the group as a whole. It strikes me that the nine-to-five commuter is actually freer in being able to pursue individual interests than a man who has, in fact, substituted one set of society's rules for another. When you commit yourself to a group, you can't take on your own projects or take off for a weekend just like that. Your time is really not your own because personal time is the only legal tender in communal living—it's the only thing you have to offer that the group needs and values.

It is usually the poverty of the ideas around which a commune is organized that has bankrupted most communal living situations. Nevertheless, in the last five years people have straggled out of the cities in sizable and silly numbers to start some kind of communal life based on the hype dream of a leader or a well-known theory. By far the most viable scheme seems to be B. F. Skinner's society Walden Two, a here-and-now concept based on technology and intellectual growth.

Back in 1948 Skinner saw the error the make-believe pioneers made in setting up primitive communities. As he says in his *Walden Two*, a rather bold piece of proselytizing thinly disguised in novel form,

> the point . . . is that we avoid the temptation to return to primitive modes of farming and industry. Communities are usually richer in manpower than in materials or cash, and this has often led to the fatal belief that there was manpower to spare. . . . Utopias usually spring from a rejection of modern life. Our point of view here isn't atavistic, however. We look ahead, not backwards, for a better version.

Indeed, probably the oldest commune, Twin Oaks, in Virginia, is based on Skinner. It has survived, but with a remarkably large turnover, the only sustaining force coming from one or maybe two of the original founders.

The other people who have drifted in and out have indeed contributed their work on a labor-credit system, where value points are given for each task that must be done. But they have contributed, then left, as if "commune" were just another phase in the development of young kids—college, graduate school, a job, then a commune. Kathleen Kinkade, a founder of Twin Oaks, even says as much when she compares commune life to the college bull session, once removed: "One *can* find interesting people in college, but how do college people sustain that kind of environment when they leave college? They've got to go out and leave that highly stimulating atmosphere. At Twin Oaks it never stops." (Kat tells all in her new book, *A Walden Two Experiment.*)

But I am getting away from the point. The main economic base for Twin Oaks is the rope-hammock business. And while that is a perfectly viable and organic product, it should have been obvious to the original founders that making rope hammocks has its own kind of assembly-line tediousness. Following the Skinnerian system of utilizing brawn as well as brains, a community had better provide plenty of alternatives to the making of rope hammocks for its members, or it won't sustain itself.

But Twin Oaks does live on, in prophecy of Skinnerian doctrine, giving rise to many other groups that hope to establish themselves along similar lines. One of these groups that is showing success in a limited way is the East Street Gallery in Grinnell, Iowa.

The town of Grinnell is like one of those places you pass through on the way to someplace else—a flat crisscross of streets with nothing to distinguish them except a formidable old bank by Louis Sullivan, done in the days when he had to go around to small Midwestern towns doing banks. Grinnell is typically small-town America and A-town except for its college, Grinnell, with its liberal and adventurous reputation. Out of the college several years ago came Henry Wilhelm and Krys Neuman, a loose couple as they call themselves (in the sense of convention, not morality), with a great interest in photography. Henry has the look of a tamed Joe Cocker about him—wild hair, perpetual grin. Krys is more serious: when she speaks it's strong and important. In 1968 they went to Washington to do a book on the Poor People's March. When they returned to Grinnell, they moved into an old house that Henry had grown up in when his father was a professor at Grinnell. Into that house they moved several friends and the equipment for making the most ingenious photographic print washer ever designed. Krys and Henry are very involved in photopermanence, and they have put the little town of Grinnell on the photographic map because of the inventiveness of their product. But more important, they have an economic base for their commune—a base born of technology, not pioneering.

The house on East Street sags and groans in protest of the unorthodox use it's being put to. I was amazed as I walked in the door at the poor use of space and the general ugliness of the house. The walls in the living room are painted black—a physical statement of their protest against society and its vulgar and inferior interior decoration. Requisite leftist posters, some in French, are stuck haphazardly to the walls. The furniture would be refused by the Salvation Army. And taped everywhere are signs that tell you you're in an experiment in living, not just somebody's home: "No dope." "Girls, don't throw Tampax in the john." In the kitchen, sagging shelves hold photographic supplies, not sugar. However, there's a microwave oven. (Wait a minute with your preconceptions—Krys and Henry do protest but this isn't a back-to-the-land movement; this is a technologically based commune.) And on the oven, crayoned on shirt cardboard, a list of rules how to use the brute.

Krys and Henry acknowledge much to Skinner and to Walden Two. Their labor-credit system covers all the work that has to be done, from production of print washers to taking out the garbage. The system is rated on a scale of desirability (not difficulty) in the community, with a required four credits a day. (For example, out of a possible four credits, working in the flower garden at Walden Two was given .1 an hour, so nice a way to pass the time was it, while cleaning the sewers had a much higher point value.)

Henry had been resented because he was working downstairs in the factory/basement for all of his credits and not helping with the housework. Eventually, the commune got a dishwasher, and Henry was so infatuated with the machine that now he does all of the dishes all of the time. (Remember that this commune is based on technology.)

In a quiet moment Krys and Henry both admitted they were growing tired of assembling the Plexiglas print washers in their undersized, low-ceilinged basement. Yet when I pressed them with the suggestion that they get a plastics manufacturer to produce the washers cheaper, and certainly faster, ideology reared its head. "We're very into good working conditions in the factory, and good hours, humane work. We'd never like to get that far away from our work. There's something immoral about just sitting back and letting royalty checks come in." The solution is to have a "factory of their own." They are negotiating to buy a building that is legitimately zoned. The only drawback is that the present owner insists on having business meetings in the morning long before Henry is usually up.

As a loose couple with a mutual affinity for each other, Krys and Henry form the nucleus of a working commune with a viable economic base in technology. But because they are the central couple, their problem is getting people to work with them who would share their interest— subscribe to their dream. It is almost as if they were the marrieds and taking in boarders. Krys and Henry have recognized this problem and insist that they will encourage personal projects of their other members and make their labor time available for someone else's dream.

Assuming that enough people get together and that a commune works out the labor-credit problems satisfactorily, there's another problem: sex. Many middle-class, middle-aged people wound up in their own marriages through a need to satisfy convention, not intimacy. Now, they lust after the supposed freedom of free love, which they think commune life must be about. Krys and Henry answer the sex question in this way: "We suspect the present-day nuclear family structure creates disturbed children and adults. We plan to replace the family structure with group living and raise children as a group— though we won't have children unless we feel the commune is stable enough for us to think it will last for a long time. (It wouldn't be good for the children otherwise.)

We will start out with individuals or 'loose couples' but not with married folk. We will keep the population equally balanced between men and women.

"Initially we will be experimenting with heterosexual relationships. As we experiment with new structures and find something we think not good, we will try something different. We will always attempt to relate what we are doing to large, technologically advanced groups of people."

Quite a manifesto, one a lot of us would like to have been able to write. But pause a minute and think of what it would be like if you just took off with a dozen of your closest friends. People in the set-and-scheduled Saturday night social plan would have a hell of a time getting together twelve compatible people—think of how it is when you try to get friends of yours to meet other friends. Whether it's jealousy or just plain obtuseness, it rarely works. Now, imagine trying to live with them. Then, think of all the couples where you like *him* but can't abide *her*. If you take him, you'll have to put up with her. Unless in the psychic trauma he loses her—which is fine, but puts a stray and searching male in your midst. Next, consider your own professional prejudices. Your evaluation of yourself in your work is implicitly based on the other person and how superior you are compared to him, or how you wish you could work, get ahead, succeed like him. It seems impossible that this evaluation based on the competitive system of doing business would just dry up and go away. The need to judge your closest friends in terms of productivity would be a terribly damaging one in practice. "I really like John but he just isn't doing his share" is not the best kind of attitude to have of a fellow

communard. Out there in the real world all our friends
do different enough work from ours that we are always
able to withhold judgment and just assume they're doing
okay at whatever it is they choose to do. But when you're
all in it together, it's a different story, and if someone isn't
baking the bread right, or often enough, it's a source of
real annoyance.

It always amazes me, in reading or hearing about communes in existence or dreamed of, that newcomers are always welcomed—even sought after. Think of how hard it
is to make and keep a really good friend. Think of the
many social levels and subtle ways we have of judging
and condemning on the basis of achievement, education,
degree of liberal thinking, or humanity. Then, to be able
to suddenly open up and accept, go with the flow, it is
downright unrealistic. Maybe the children of Twin Oaks
will be able to do it, maybe those of East Street, maybe
the children even of our attempts will be able to strip
away the old attitudes about monogamy and judgmental
criteria, and "experiment with heterosexual relationships." I wonder. Though I sincerely wish it, I secretly
don't believe we can.

Homesteading

Know what a farm is? It's what a city man dreams
of at 5 P.M., but never at 5 A.M.—*Waupun* (Wis.)
Leader News

My husband and I were sitting one night with old
friends in our favorite New York French restaurant, a

place that is expensive enough to have class but not expensive enough to have insolence.

At one point during dinner the male friend leaned over to me and said, "We're going to try homesteading."

I did not respond, really, but reached for my wine glass. "Well, what do you think?" he asked.

He wasn't kidding.

"That could be terrific," I answered as enthusiastically as possible, "but what do you mean exactly by 'homesteading'?"

"Well, we have this land," he began, and as he talked, I sipped the wine he had so carefully ordered and tested with much sniffing of cork and appraising of color.

". . . and we'll just live off our own place, grow our own food, try to make whatever we need instead of buying it. Like that," he concluded. He looked at me intently and asked, "What do you think?" as he examined his seafood crepe.

It's always difficult to know how to start when you're questioning people's dreams, so I took first things first. "How are you going to make money?"

"We won't need much money, we'll make what we can, do our own repairs. I figure we can sell the extra vegetables we raise."

"Then you'll have a lot of land?"

"No, just enough for us to work."

"Believe me," I said, trying not to be peremptory, "you'll need quite a bit to grow your own food plus enough to sell for a decent income."

"You really don't believe me when I say we won't need much money, do you?"

He was becoming a bit defensive, so I simply said,

"Yes, I do, but I guess it depends on how much is not much." Then I smiled and hoped he'd change the subject.

His wife, Jane, interrupted. "Peter, there's Ron and Rosemary Fortune. They're just sitting down."

Peter raised his hand. "Hi Ron, Rosemary. Join us later for brandy."

The salad came, asparagus vinaigrette.

"God, what a taste," Peter said. "And just imagine growing asparagus ourselves," he said to Jane. Then to me, "When we're homesteading."

At least the mood was light, so I said, "Of course you'll have to wait three or four years for asparagus."

"Oh they grow quicker than that."

"Well, if you want to pay enough, you can buy more mature plants that will produce in two years."

"You can't discourage me. I still think we can take our savings and get a start homesteading. I'll work the heavy crops and Jane can grow herbs. There's money in that."

"And how will you market the stuff?" I asked. "Will you truck it to a town or set up a roadside stand?"

"A stand, I guess," he said, watching the waiter serve a fantastic gigot, "although our land is really nowhere near a main road."

We were interrupted by the appearance of Madame, the restaurant's proprietor. "Is everything all right, m'sieur?" she asked.

"*Très bien,*" Peter answered.

"And how is your little baby?" she asked with that particularly endearing French solicitousness.

Without hesitation, Peter produced a picture of his recent firstborn son. "He looks exactly like m'sieur," she teased, and Peter smiled through his fashionably trimmed beard like a benevolent Santa Claus.

Madame moved to another table, and as Peter put away the picture he said, "And we're going to get that kid away from this city and out on the land where he can live and breathe."

"Now that's a good idea," I said. "I couldn't agree more."

"But you don't think we can make it homesteading. Right?"

"Wrong. I just don't want you to go into it with some romanticized notion of what it will be like. You'll need money. Maybe not much, but enough for doctor bills, food you can't grow, especially the first year—and admit it, wouldn't you want enough bread to come into town for a great French meal once in a while?"

"I guess," he said.

"Let me tell you just one story and we'll drop it, okay?"

"Okay."

I said, "We have a couple of friends who were living out on the land and commuting to their jobs in town. They had a garden, just for their own pleasure. Like everyone else, they overplanted the first year. They canned quite a bit and talked about trying to sell some produce, but never quite did it. Then one day, in the supermarket, they called on the produce manager and asked if he would be interested in buying some of their fresh herbs, in pots. Yes he would, he said, and immediately placed a long-distance call to clear the deal with his regional manager.

"My friends were ecstatic. The produce guy told them

he would take small individual herb plants on consignment, paying them 60 percent of retail, or 35 and a half cents; or he would buy them outright wholesale for $.29. They agreed to begin in the spring.

"Later at home, my friends made a list of what they'd need and started planning. Then, almost as an afterthought, they made a little revenue projection and were astounded and damned discouraged when they realized they'd have to sell 20,000 little potted herbs to make $5800 gross on the wholesale deal. They could make a little more on consignment, but it's much more risky."

Peter shook his head. "Twenty thousand is a lot of herbs for six grand."

"You have the picture," I said.

"But the Nearings did it," he persisted.

"The Nearings are *writers*. They've written dozens of books. So they got money from that, plus they were in the maple-sugar business. Don't you remember, in the book . . ."

"I never got to read the book. Every time I go to the library it's out."

Finding a piece of land far out and a little house is probably the most highly charged dream of our times. When we are so disconnected from the source of the food we eat, and, more important, unsure and insecure about our abilities to survive in the basic living state, there is a compelling need to return to the land. We want to perform the very basic living chores for ourselves, maybe to prove that we're alive after all.

The homesteading dream is always hazy: lazy, like

mending a harness in the noonday sun, never feeding the horses; digging around in a row of potatoes only when you feel like it; spending whole days making soap, or candles, or love. The only trouble is that it's also necessary to make money. And since the move to homesteading is precisely a reaction against such crassness, making money just isn't in the plan. But just as bad as disdain for the dollar is the prevalent notion of going back to the land as they did in the nineteenth century, without electricity, machinery, or sophisticated techniques that have already been discovered.

When we were kids, we would go down to the basement of our house, turn out the lights, throw blankets over the windows, drag out bridge tables, and drape them with blankets to make tents. Each of us had a candle, and on mysterious, whispered signals, we'd make sneaky sorties to the spooky back-room canned-goods closet, loading our arms with the unopened cans and hoard them back in the tent, against the time, I guess, when the house upstairs would blow away. Sitting there in the afternoon darkness, with only blankets for walls and candles for light, the whole superstructure of the house above us and the world around us disappeared in our intensity of belief in this new state of being we had made.

But after a while it would be time to blow out the candles, return the canned peaches, and put the blankets back upstairs on our beds. The first electric light we turned on was more than a shock to our eyes—it was the confusion of worlds you get when you stumble outside after a movie. When crude reality intrudes on the private little universe you had let yourself believe in.

Homesteaders who set out for the land with only the clothes on their back and a few tools may find the shelter of the dark ages, but they are *pretending* not to be in the middle of a technological society. The most disturbing thing about this arbitrary make-believe is that you may be safe and secure under a blanket tent but you're *in* a pine-paneled basement.

Helen and Scott Nearing (who got out to Vermont in 1932, then recently moved to Maine as civilization discovered Vermont) are undoubtedly the current heroes of the homesteading movement. They have indeed led a model life off the land. But the thing that strikes me as unrealistic about their code, as described in their book *Living the Good Life*, is this:

> Our pattern for the simple life did not include ice-box, refrigerator or freezing unit. We aimed to work out alternatives which would provide us with the foods we wanted, at the time we wanted them, and still leave us comparatively free of the power interests and merchandizers of large-scale gadgets.

So, with this arbitrary decision against a mechanical foodkeeper, and already committed to producing and storing their own food, "the vegetables tended to rot" for several seasons before they had a stone root cellar built. Blankets and bridge tables again. To suffer a loss of food, which really means a loss of energy and production, for a principle against capitalism, when for a very small amount of money you could buy a used box and supply it with ice and keep food, is unnecessary hardship and has the ring of self-inflicted martyrdom about it. And it does seem to me that the letters I've gotten from the Nearings are written on a typewriter, which is as close as anything to the power interests and merchandisers of large-scale gadgets. You're splitting hairs between Smith-Corona and Frigidaire.

A younger disciple of the Nearings has been portrayed to me by a mutual friend as "spending all day digging out a tree stump when if he had thrown a chain around the bumper of his jeep [which he still keeps], it would have taken only minutes." And using wood instead of electricity for heat and light uses up more fossil fuel than does electricity.

Granted, a return to the land is a reaction against blind progress and the gross perpetuation of technology to the detriment of man. But *pretending* that there aren't better ways of doing things than those of the pretechnological dark ages is make-believe basement stuff. Worse, it takes away all the freedom one left society to seek. Why spend a whole day at a task when with a little ingenuity (instead of sentimental and antique artifice) you can get the work done and be free to live, really live on the land you love.

Hawthorne, who seemed really to have been there, says in *Blithedale*:

The peril of our new way of life was not lest we should fail in becoming practical agriculturists, but that we should probably cease to be anything else. . . . The clods of earth, which we so constantly belabored and turned over and over, were never etherealized into thought. Our thoughts, on the contrary, were fast becoming cloddish.

Scott and Helen Nearing knew this, that the land, as well as technology, can take away your freedom to think and to create. They very meticulously left at least four hours a day for their personal pursuits—Scott's writing, Helen's writing and her music.

Their book, *Living the Good Life*, has become a bible of our time. But before you get carried away with what you've heard about blueberries as big as quarters, a kitchen redolent with herbs hand grown, fresh fruit juices, sweet nutmeat cakes, and a house of stone they built themselves, understand that the Nearings have gone about the business of homesteading like the social scientists they are—with scrupulous planning, almost maniacal attention to detail, all the standard operating procedures and five-year plans endemic to that dread world from which they came.

I asked the Nearings, Helen now sixty-four, and Scott eighty-seven, what they would recommend for people who were now trying to leave the system and Live their Good Life. Their answers—responsible and tough—follow, with, I hope, cures for the innocent who would walk among his fields to never think on the evils of money again.

Here are some suggestions and advice for newcomers to the simple life:

1. Be sure your overhead costs (taxes, rent, interest, etc.) are well within limits of prospective income after making the change.

2. You should have enough backlog of capital to live for a minimum of three years (after you've

bought your place) without any income from cash
crops.

3. Make the change gradually, if this will assist
in your venture. Secure the land while continuing
on your job. If any improvements have to be made,
spread them over the first year of ownership. If your
prospective country place is within reasonable traveling distance of your work place, move into the
country the second year and commute to work. By
the third year, if all goes well, you'll be getting at
least food and shelter from your country place, as
well as some income from your cash crops. By that
time you will have learned the ropes and will be
able to give up your job and settle down in the
country without a sudden break.

4. The kind of a life we are living is much easier
for two people than for a single person. If you have
a family with two or three growing children who
live at home, be sure to interest them in the venture
and secure their cooperation. With three or four
people taking a real interest in the new venture, and
with moderately good management, you can hardly
fail to build up a workable economy.

Surprisingly capitalistic terms for the "leftist" Nearings. But they've been through it and they know that living off the land involves a rigorous discipline and a pretty
infallible way of earning a living. Cash flow can't just
stop.

The Nearings went to homesteading in the thirties.
Are their ideas and procedures different from those of

people turning to the homestead forty years later? Not very.

Michele and John McCaffrey have everything one needs to make it homesteading: they have a house and garden that hug a hillside along the well-traveled Route 5 in Putney, Vermont; they have a fully stocked organic- and health-food shop in the house; *and* they have a job. Or John does. While Michele runs the shop at home, John works as an accountant for the nearby Experiment in International Living.

On their land are two huge gardens with all the basic vegetables, a grape arbor, comfrey patch, and herb garden. Plus some chickens and a family of goats.

The McCaffreys were just getting into organic eating when they left New York City (he managed bookstores, unhappily) and moved to Putney. In 1968, the first year, they harvested so many tomatoes they didn't know what to do. So they set up a little table by the road with a sign, Organic Tomatoes. In a day they were sold, and the McCaffreys knew there was money in health. Understand that Putney is not just your back-roads Vermont town. For years it has been the summer place of many New York and Boston folk who have gradually moved there for good. Also, it's the home of the well-known progressive Putney Summer Work Camp, where the upper-middle-class intelligentsia send their kids to get the proper mix of poetry and elbow grease. (Said one mother, "All my thirteen-year-old learned was how to swear and how to paint someone else's barn. For a thousand dollars, she could have learned that at home.")

At any rate, it's entirely feasible that something as timely as organic vegetables and natural foods would find acceptance in Putney. Little by little, the McCaffreys expanded their roadside business. The next year they purposely planted a surplus of vegetables they knew they could sell. Michele dried her own leaves for tea (sassafras, raspberry, strawberry) and learned to make yogurt and various pastes and slaws in her blender, which is as essential to organic eating as a mimeograph machine is to any underground cause. Before long, customers were driving from many miles around. The McCaffreys founded the Bungaree Health Food Store in a corner of their kitchen and finally, in 1972, added a whole wing to their house as a shop where they sell nationally marketed health foods, like Tiger's Milk, as well as their own preparations.

Every cent John makes from his accounting work is turned right back into the store and garden, with the hope that very soon he can quit the outside work altogether, get several dozen laying hens and more goats, and be able to make it on the store and farm alone.

The only excess that I could see to the McCaffreys' homesteading operation is that they are into the health-food cult to such an extent that they live and breathe organic food. They are now completely vegetarian, and their youngest son, almost one year old, has never eaten meat. Also they believe cooking is chemically wrong, for it kills all the helpful bacteria. One evening meal I observed consisted of one slice of tomato, a piece of cheese, a mound of cabbage slaw, and a glass of goat's milk. It wasn't what they were eating, but the austere portions that tended to boggle the stomach of the observer.

Eccentricities aside, the McCaffreys have a sound and workable farm business that could be adapted in many other parts of this country. They say, "We find the most common misconception people have about homesteading today is that they can start with no money and become completely independent financially by just living off the land. Common sense should dictate otherwise. They try to make do with the minimum of food and medical attention while doing hard manual work from dawn to dusk. We have even seen cases of severe malnutrition, scurvy, and dysentery among some young people. They grow organic vegetables, but don't eat them themselves—they take them to market to sell. They literally kill themselves to prove a theory which doesn't work unless the most ideal conditions exist."

The five things the McCaffreys would suggest to people contemplating homesteading are:

1. Start with enough money to provide yourselves with the following basic requirements for two years:
   - The outright purchase of property or money to cover payments on same for two years
   - Mortgage and taxes
   - Animals, seeds, equipment
   - Freezer and root cellar
   - Clothing
   - Allowance for medical and dental treatment, etc., especially accidents
   - An extra cushion of at least $2000 to cover hidden expenses (believe me, they exist).

2. Don't jump into homesteading. Work toward it in gradual stages. Many homesteading skills can and should be pursued while still in the city. Most are time-consuming to learn and involve the pur-

chase of equipment and supplies. A partial list of
the skills good to know are:
- First aid, swimming, carpentry, woodlore (including recognizing wild foods and medicines),
  hunting (gun and bow), organic gardening, and
  farming (animals, etc.)
- Primitive cooking, breadmaking, etc.
- Crafts associated with homesteading.

  3. Take trips to wilderness areas to adjust to the
atmosphere gradually.

  4. Have a plan, organize your work, and discipline yourself.

  5. Work toward developing an extra source of income separate or related to the homestead.

  6. Don't do it because it's now the style. Homesteading in its purest state taxes all the senses, the
mind, and the spirit. It takes character to do it and
survive. The people involved should be mature,
well-balanced, and compatible with each other.

It is significant that the Nearings, approaching homesteading as the only viable way to live in this country,
and the McCaffreys, coming to it as the only viable way
to eat, should both underscore the need for a kind of discipline that one doesn't automatically associate with just
finding a piece of land and living off it.

8

The New Work Ethic

There will never be any *new* places to get out to. We simply have to change our ideas about the old ones. In the same way, if we reject the traditional social evaluations of jobs (working in a hardware store is not a suitable occupation for a college graduate), it opens up a whole range of possible ways to make money. Getting out is, after all, a rejection of society's rules of the game. Like the kid running away from home who doesn't have to worry anymore about not being allowed to cross the street, there must be an accompanying rejection of the stigma about the ways this game should be played.

The system stratifies a man by what he does, not by

how he does it or by what he is. These criteria don't leave
much room for humanity. In this supposedly classless society the broad middle class has many subtle levels: we
have rigid and pernicious ideas about what is suitable, as
if we were raising Edwardian gentlemen. Take teaching
as an example. It is perfectly acceptable, even honorable,
for a man to become a college professor, but the publish-
or-perish doctrine is held to as rigorously by his peers
who judge him as by his superiors. He is expected to
move on and up in the academic world in a political bat-
tle as fierce as that at IBM. Should he become disenchanted with the upper academe, the alternatives in
teaching are very limited. Opting for teaching on any
lesser education level has its accompanying loss of class
(status). Junior college just isn't *serious* enough. High
school is a step down, but okay if it's a New England
prep school or a New York private school where frantic
parents try to enroll their children at birth. Anything elementary is just that, suitable only for limited (i.e., lower-
middle-class) fellows. And women Ph.D.'s.

It's just like the corporate sales structure. A young and
enthusiastic sales trainee is sent into a territory with a
senior man. The young guy's turned on about the product and soon he has his own territory. He's making
pretty good money and he's good at what he does. His
next step, however, is back to the office as some regional
sales director, and he's not selling, he's administrating.
This is the logical promotion, but it doesn't give him the
kick selling did. If he remained on the selling force, he'd
eventually be written off as having no ambition at all and
he'd become the oldest salesman in the company.

A newspaper article datelined Normal, Illinois, has

this headline: "Give Up Life of Books to Be an Auto Mechanic." It's the story of an Illinois State University librarian, thirty-eight, with a master's degree, who dug books "only when they pertained to auto mechanics." With the understanding approval of his family, he is forsaking the library for the garage. What's neat about this story is that we all know the social pressure that led him to become a librarian instead of an auto mechanic in the first place.

Job connotations are changing today, however. Gradually, as our discomfiture and panic at creeping technocracy grows, it has become more acceptable to be an artisan. Over the last few years it has become okay to become a carpenter, provided, of course, that you are executing your own designs, or at least Parsons tables. Working in someone else's shop and mass-producing shutters or Early American kitchen cabinets is still, however, considered menial. It is also suddenly acceptable to be an old-fashioned craftsman, depending, of course, on what materials you use. Being a leathersmith, a potter, a weaver is appreciated in the light of integrity of the materials—and the acceptability of working with one's hands. So a children's book editor at Random House can get out and become a potter in a little town in New Hampshire without any loss of status. It still is *infra dig* to practice a craft like watch repair. That is, it's all right to tool a leather strap but not to mess with the works.

The academe who leaves the library for the garage is more readily accepted now than he would have been ten years ago. But it wouldn't have been too cool had he become an auto mechanic just out of high school or college. It's a trade-off of principles: in place of the requirements for income or social respectability is a new respect for personal commitment and fulfillment.

But if our job criteria are opening up a bit, it's not because of a rejection of expertise or an endorsement of manual labor that rejects education. We're not talking about the Ph.D. who drives a taxi as a way out. The idea is rather to forget about what is traditionally acceptable. It's a plea to find occupations that have always been considered pedestrian or prosaic and to invest them with new energy—jobs that when completed leave time for new freedoms. The idea is to choose businesses that, infused with your own knowledge, become something else altogether, even as the small town becomes a different place to live with the sophistication and enthusiasm of the middle-class professional.

When a New York media salesman opens up a Dunkin' Donuts shop in Connecticut, it's going to be with a different attitude than the man down the street who saved and slaved for years to buy a franchise. The media man has new options: his own small business to experiment with instead of giving his time and life to *Time* and *Life*; or it may just be an easy way of making a living, leaving him time for the rest of his life. Or he may like doughnuts a lot. Any way he chooses to play it, he has removed the traditional occupational stigma.

In the same way, a man who takes a job, any job, just to be in a beautiful leisure area is the up-to-date, responsible version of the traditional ski bum. He works hard at being a janitor or a gas-station attendant so he can take off to go skiing three or four times a week.

Life in the system, because there are vacations and

more Things, may have the appearance of increased leisure time. But that appearance is a mirage.

People who get out are still strong and active and long
ago stopped believing the myth that with increased
affluence we are headed toward Leisure City. The highly
touted four-day work week, which will never mean anything to professionals or executives, has been misinter-
preted: it's not really a way to allow people to work less.
It's a way to get machines to work more. Like all indus-
trial reform, it is actually a move toward greater
efficiency: two shifts *perform* better in fewer stints of longer
hours.

The Harried Leisure Class, Staffan Linder's thorough
study of the use of our time, says that all time falls into
four categories: work time, personal time, culture time,
and consumption time. Of the four, the last is the most
significant. No matter how many things we buy for leisure use, we cannot use all of them at once. We have a
fixed amount of time to use an increasing number of
goods. When we buy things to use in leisure time, we do
not consider the time it takes to use them. Linder calls
this "pleasure blindness." Also when buying, we seldom
add in the time it takes to keep these things working. Linder calls this "maintenance blindness."

There is a man I know who has just the right combination of finance and fantasy to be able to buy all the
strange and wonderful things he fancies. Each item is for
him a way of getting out while staying in—the theoretical maximum use of leisure time. He is too infinitely original to crave the ordinary spoils of wealth. But consider
his dilemma. First, he bought a great old house in the

country, overlooking a river (a railroad, too, but a river). The house was perfect except that it needed a lot of work so that each weekend was spent rebuilding and rewiring. Then, he saw a wonderful old car (a 1939 Packard touring car) he just had to have, which was okay except that it took him two wonderful old hours more to get to the repair job on the great old house each weekend. Then, as luck would have it, he had a chance to buy an incredible old boat, which resembled the car in condition. He reasoned, however, that it had the advantage of being able to travel on water, so, he could make the trip to the country house without traffic. Except there was the hassle of getting the boat ready each Friday and closing it down each Sunday. Of course, in winter neither the wonderful old car nor the incredible old boat could make the trip to the great old house. So, he was obliged to buy yet another means of transportation, and shunning the idea of a tacky new car, he bought a fifteen-year-old Rolls Royce, assured by its owner to be in fine working condition. Which was true except that the bottom had rusted out.

The trouble with leisure is that we have such little time to do each thing, we wind up playing so hard it's work. Johan Huizinga's book on play, *Homo Ludens* ("man the player"), says that the play element in culture has been on the wane since the eighteenth century. He implies further that today's competitive team sports and games like chess are too serious (the main criterion for play being nonseriousness), too professional, and too intellectual to be played at. There are endless statistics to prove that we spend most of our so-called play time as spectators of nonplay sports, twice-removed by television. And lest we find too much relaxation in that, the business of watching and playing these sports has become deadly serious and scientific. As one friend said, "It used to be that they gave the quarterback the ball and with any luck at all, he got rid of it. Now it is all strategies and analysis—work."

Even when they get away from television, sportsmen work: weekend golfers can't stay out late because they have to go on the course at 4:30 A.M. to beat the waiting time, and then they play thirty-six instead of eighteen holes, so difficult is it to get to play.

Sailing is potentially the purest sport—a piece of cloth and a boat against the vagaries of the wind. It should be a great and carefree emotional release. Instead, as soon as a sailor learns to handle his boat, he joins a club and gets into the racing game. He worries about his equipment, trying to afford all the newest and lightest equipment so he can *win*.

In 1970, 40,000,000 people trailered or tented out in this country's 500,000 camping places. Does this mean a quiet and relaxing time, or is this leisure indistinguishable from the frantic rest of life? Life on a trailer is just like life at home, only smaller. Trailer camps are an easy satire on the difficulties we have getting away from it all, equipped as they are with television antennas, both kinds of running water, shops, and bars, all on joyless, viewless plots jammed with other trailers, with no more room than a parking lot.

The weird thing that occurs in yacht basins is that boat owners come down to their interior-decorated boats for the weekend with a case of beer and a barbecue and never leave their mooring. This is not a particularly American phenomenon. In the chic French port of St.-Tropez, yachts are parked in such a way that they couldn't get out if they wanted to. Thorstein Veblen, who called it "conspicuous leisure," long ago had the last word.

What a sad and neurotic group we are who have so many toys there's no time left for play; whose play is so contrived and hassled it's more like work; who keep reassuring ourselves that Out Day Will Come, and when it does, we spend it shopping.

The Gotten Out have solved many of the problems by moving to the great outdoors, where they have leisure activities close at hand. If skiing is a positive pleasure, they'll go where it's accessible, saving the wearing hours of driving to and from. (In fact, this very routine—the exhilaration of skiing, then the inevitable downer of a six-hour drive home—has caused many exhausted people to see the light and get out. Their impulse is not to drop out and ski all the time, but to put themselves in a place where the skiing is easy.)

For as much as they need to relax, urban refugees want to work (of course they *have* to work, but that's something else). The strange thing about employment on the basis of personal, not social, fulfillment is that to a person all of those I interviewed work more, not less, by choice. Especially if they're in business for themselves. It's not that they don't like work, it's that they didn't like work in the workaday world.

Most of the Gotten Out put themselves in businesses that are traditionally lower-class—goods and services, mostly services. It is one of the endless ironies that in a society where you can theoretically hire people to do almost anything for you what you get is mostly theoretical.

Repairmen seldom show; maintenance people barely maintain. To feed and rest yourself, the alternatives have come to uninspired mediocrity—Howard Johnson's and Holiday Inn.

Though we have a lot of people in the service business today, the number has, obviously, nothing to do with quality or with pride.

What could be more natural, then, when this country is crying for things to be done for it, than for the accomplished professionals to get into service businesses? Furthermore, there is a tight correlation between the places people want to get out to and the work they can do there—the places are havens of natural beauty, and the work, therefore, is oriented to the people who visit the areas. Tourism—the quintessential service business. Waiting on tables, manning the cash register, washing dishes, sweeping floors—even when you own the business—is traditionally the work of the lower classes. Yet running the small businesses, shops, inns, restaurants are natural occupations for the Gotten Out.

Because of their professional experience, the Gotten Out who run restaurants, for example, don't run them in the traditional manner. Rather, they come to it with a radically different perspective—of having been somewhere else. Nor does the position of having to serve the public depress them, because they operate a restaurant the way *they* would like a restaurant to be run. Such restaurants usually have better food more lovingly prepared than this country's most chic and expensive eateries, because the owners are the cooks, or at least they eat there. Inns have more warmth and taste than almost any hotel because the owners live there. Because greater efficiency and more dollars are not the sole objects, the life-style is always better. These service businesses are an extension of the personality of the owners, a framework for them to express their styles. In a strange way, this personal and warm attention usually makes the business successful, where Harvard Business School "decision trees" would wither and fade away. Gene and Mary Foushee, who own Recapture Lodge in Bluff, Utah, say that people come back year after year. Those who first came as guests now return as close friends. "But we have no illusions about this business," Mary adds. "One of our friends is a management consultant and wanted to do a feasibility study on us. 'Don't be ridiculous,' I told him, 'we know this isn't feasible,' " says she with a great good-natured laugh.

Another thing people get from a service business is a sense of identity they might have lost in the corporate structure, where a job description sometimes takes pages, but can't be defined in a couple of words. I was talking with an art director of a big magazine about this, and he said that a job as seemingly concrete as his was often impossible for people to understand. "People ask me, 'What do you do?' and I say, 'I'm an art director.' And they say, 'Oh, you do the drawings for the magazine?' and I say, 'No, I have illustrators for that.' So they say, 'Well, then you take the pictures,' and I say, 'No, we hire photographers.' Then, exasperated, they say, 'Well, you must decide what goes where on each page,' and I, embarrassed, admit we have three graphic designers for layouts."

A sales marketing manager in Chicago often brought home geographical maps on which he would shade in areas, apportioning them to different salesmen. When his daughter was asked in school what her father did, she replied, "Oh, he colors maps."

It's not that we can't cope with complexity too vague for a child to understand. It is that jobs that evade ready definitions are often ill-conceived and difficult to perform in practice. Most corporate management structures are glutted with titles for which there are no real jobs, and jobs without real titles.

9

Service Professions

What is it really like to leave corporate insurance on Wall Street and get into a service business like an inn in Maine?

It takes so long to get to Christmas Cove, Maine, once you've turned off the road from Damariscotta, that you have a lot of time to fantasize about what the Coveside Inn will be like. As you go deeper into the heavily wooded land that keeps closing in on the little road, the inn becomes smaller and more rustic in your anticipation. When you dip down the hill into the tiny fishing town that sits just before the island that is the Cove, you're sure of its simplicity. There's only a tiny food store and a lot of seagulls in South Bristol. Crossing the bridge and pressing on still farther through more woods, your image of the inn has now shrunk to some kind of homestead shack with a couple of bedrooms upstairs. Rounding the last bend, you come upon Coveside Inn, totally unprepared, of course, for what you see. There on the hill is a majestic old dowager of a New England building, fronting her warm red saltbox facade to the sea. At the bottom of the hill, in the suburbs of her pleasure, is a string of motel units opening onto a front porch that literally hangs over the water. Nestled farther along the cove are other low red wooden buildings that turn out to be a dining room and gift shop, and a grocery store built around a dock. Beyond the dock a dozen boats are moored, secure in the sheltered harbor made by the small outlying islands that protect the shore from the Atlantic beyond.

We walked into the bar attached to the dining room, and seeing a man behind it asked, "Are you Mike Mitchell?"

"No," he answered, "but I wish I were."

When we finally did sit down with Mike and Barbara Mitchell it was a day later. We had glimpsed them in the dining room, in the lobby of the old house, on the dock, and selling groceries. Mike was always talking quietly with guests from the boats or the inn.

Mike Mitchell is in his early forties; his hair is close-cropped and his voice is rough from the tens of thousands of cigarettes that must have preceded his perpetual pipe. Whenever the Mitchells do get a chance to sit on their front porch they can overlook their little empire, the broad front lawn with mighty trees, the smaller buildings, the harbor beyond. The Mitchells are in the fourth year of their endeavor and say that they made some money in 1972.

(Without knowing it, Mike has proved the economic theory of the Gotten Out advanced by a compatriot, Bob Ballard of the Weston Village Store, and predicts, "The first year you'll lose money. The second year, you'll probably break even, and the third year, you'll begin to show a profit. Now if someone tells you this little formula, as someone told me, you'll automatically say, 'Hell, I can do better than that, I'm a lot smarter.' But you have no idea of the mistakes you can make. Showing a profit in the third year begins to look pretty damn good.")

"The first year," Mitchell is saying, "we were ridiculous to even open. We moved in April and the buildings were peeling old white paint and the previous owners had let the plumbing go to hell. But we got a seventy-four-year-old man to do the painting and got the plumbing to work minimally. The only structural change we made was to add the bar. When we opened the restaurant the first night, word of mouth had brought in a lot of boats and a lot of curious neighbors. We had seventy people in the dining room. Barb was the hostess with not an experienced waiter in the lot of kids. Wow! No wonder we didn't even break even the first year.

"You know," he continued, "this may sound contrary to my Wall Street insurance background, but good planning isn't necessarily the key to success in this business. I mean in our restaurant all the vegetables we serve are from little local gardens. Now we could save money buying in bulk but we don't want to. We just set up a place that we'd like to go to."

The Mitchells' year has a definite pattern. Their season runs from about May to early October. Apart from the inn, a good part of their business is in boats and service. They haul and store boats for the winter, and it's Christmas by the time all that is done. Extensive repairs to the inn are made during the winter. Last year Mike tore apart the main living room and redid it. In March they start to put the inn together again, and another season begins.

The Mitchells' children, two sons and a daughter, are part of the operation. During the summer, the boys work on the dock, ferrying newspapers and doughnuts out to the twenty-three moorings every morning, working around the boats in the day. One morning I saw the fifteen-year-old son, Mark, repeatedly dive off the dock and untangle a rope from around some guy's propeller, which is not a bad way for kids to grow up.

Mike has been around boats all his life, in his early years on Martha's Vineyard and then sailing the Long Island Sound from suburban Rowayton (from which they got out). He's been in six Bermuda races and knows his way around. "Yet," he says, "it's funny when a guy will come in to the dock and I'll start tying up his boat and he'll say, 'You'd better let me do that.' Or, 'On the Sound we do it this way, but you wouldn't know about that.' But what the hell, I keep telling myself I'm in a service business, and it doesn't bother me. We meet some wonderful people here. And all our friends have been up to see us."

Barbara, with her close-cropped hair and crew-neck sweater, joins us and warns Mike, "Better not say we love everything. In the beginning we worked eighteen hours a day, and I can't say I loved that."

Mike, when pressed, admitted he hated hauling garbage and going to faraway Rockland for ice. "I get sick of what's broken down and try to figure out how we can hang on until the season ends. And then we have total no privacy. But I guess we have to accept that."

Says Barbara, "It's much better than a regime for the sake of it. In the summer, the family doesn't eat a single meal together. We all have different jobs and different schedules. But in the winter we're always together. We don't go out much, unless it's with the children, and if we have people in, we all have dinner together."

Part of Barbara's work is running the gift shop. And she's successful at that, Mike feels, because she has never been a buyer before. "After I learned that I had to have stuff for people who didn't have the same taste as I do, it went fine." But Mike feels there's something healthy and invigorating about going about a discipline in an untrained way: what you bring to it is your native intelligence and your experience; you need not have done it before.

I asked him my favorite question, "Isn't leaving the insurance business and getting into this business just trading one set of problems for another?"

"The problems here," Mike said, "I can reach out and grab ahold of. It's not like business problems, where you grind your gut about some vice-president in a meeting. Here, I know what physically has to be done, and if I don't feel like it today I can say, 'Oh the hell with it, I've got tomorrow.' I know the pressures here will never get me the way they did on Wall Street." On Wall Street the pressures so got to Mike Mitchell (not a habitually violent man) that in his last weeks he ripped the phone from the wall and punched a man.

Far across the country, in a setting much more Alpine than New England, is a man who left Boston to run an inn. Bob Graham, in Jackson Hole, Wyoming, echoes Mike Mitchell's sentiments. "The problems you have are different here. I get up in the morning and the sky is cobalt blue and somehow problems don't matter. They don't get to me. I used to come home on Friday and not unwind until Saturday afternoon, and then Sunday I would start crunching up again. Here, I work ten, twelve, fourteen hours a day and the day is full and I'm not tired, and then we'll take off for the mountains and picnic."

How Bob Graham left his job as sales and marketing manager for two Boston electronic firms is a tale of almost Dickensian coincidence. He was on an airplane to Washington, D.C., and just happened to sit next to Jackson Hole's booster and manager, Buzz Bainbridge, who suggested that Bob come out on his next vacation and have a look. Bob, who figured he averaged driving six to ten thousand miles a year to go skiing out of Boston, loved what he saw—the little *nouveau*-Swiss village of Jackson Hole with nothing but ski trails for backyard. He wistfully queried Bainbridge, who just happened to know about the managership of a ski lodge that just happened to be open. "Here," said Buzz, "here's the phone, call in your resignation." It took Bob Graham only three weeks to make the decision and move; his wife, Kris, was all for it. "We sold all we couldn't carry and left the rest."

The Crystal Springs Inn, which Bob manages, is owned by a vice-president of Standard Oil of New Jersey. That means, in some ways, Bob has it easier than someone in business for himself. Although his salary is based on the occupancy of the inn (which means he's got to do a lot of selling), he is guaranteed some income and doesn't have to put all his capital into a business. He does have an option to buy the inn someday. In the two years since he and Kris have been in Jackson Hole, they've bought a share in eight condominium units, which they manage, with more in the works. Bob is very active in a new resort association, which will allow all the Jackson Hole inns and hotels to work together.

Bob says having money in their first year helped a lot. "But it was less than a third of what we had back East. Kris was a schoolteacher, now she's a bartender in the inn across the way. We paid our debts in Boston and then we tore up our credit cards. We haven't regretted that we cut off that link with civilization. You come out here with the idea that you're going to accept less, but that less is worth a lot more."

The Grahams have a couple of horses and a four-wheel-drive jeep and do a lot of backcountry camping, when Bob can get away from the inn and Kris can leave the little bar she mans twelve hours a day, seven days a week during the season.

Kris is in her late twenties, and Bob is about ten years older. They are part of a smooth young group who are working and living in Jackson Hole. "Right now," Kris says, "we're all sort of struggling. And we're very honest with each other. We can't afford to have conflicts—we're living so closely together." It's a case of tourism bringing about a fine sense of community. Both Kris and Bob are studying for real estate brokers' licenses, a field many of the Gotten Out get into. It is a little crass in that it's going back to the land to sell it. But more of that later.

The Mitchells bought an already existing, albeit shaky inn, Bob Graham walked into a ready managership, but Gene and Mary Foushee fell in love with the country and saw building a motel as the only way they could stay there.

Gene Foushee is a North Carolina boy whose father took him to Utah as a child. "He ruined me for corporate life," says Gene, who left Union Carbide over ten years ago and came to Bluff, Utah, with his wife and daughter. Gene, then in his early thirties, was convinced he could build a motel—he'd done some construction work back home in North Carolina. He was also convinced of another thing: The New Road was going through Bluff. And with The New Road bringing tourists through the town, a motel was the very thing. The New Road was to continue the main tourist route through Mesa Verde National Park in southwestern Colorado through the southeast corner of Utah, and Bluff, on the way to Monument Valley, and into the Hopi Indian reservation in northeastern Arizona.

Gene spread a giant road map of the three states on the rough wood floor of Recapture Lodge and with long fingers traced the logical route The New Road would have followed. But it is now ten years later and The New Road did not go through Bluff. It did not go through Utah at all, and the remorse Gene Foushee felt in that, telling me about it a decade later, was the echo of disillusionment with the Golden West that every prospector and speculator and small businessman staking his hopes on the Railroad must have felt. But the Foushees have far too much spirit and resourcefulness to be put down by a mere government decision.

Slowly they built what is now a rustic and charming lodge. The main building has double-height ceilings (with sunlight pouring in from high windows), light wood and Indian blankets, and a long stretch of maple for a table that could seat a couple dozen.

The first year they built five units, every evening putting in a bit of paneling, and on Christmas Day, a wall.

With the ill-turned New Road many miles away, the Foushees knew they needed something else to bring in the money. Gene reasoned, "Well, if you're going to be in the tourist business, you might as well tell them what's here. I am a trained geologist and I figured I could be a tour guide, and long before ecology was in, I saw that I could offer something different. But it wasn't easy. There was a big tour operator out of Monticello who thought he owned all this country. I had to have a hearing to try and get a permit which the big guys fought all along. 'Look,' I tried to tell them, 'I am a geologist, I have a whole different story to tell than these guys who are giving "cowboy tours" of the Old West and are way off base on the factual stuff.' "

"The night before the hearings," Mary continues with a chuckle, "I had to type Gene's statement by kerosene lamp, wearing a baseball cap to shield my eyes." They got the permit. With the nature of their business changed, they could meet a light plane at any nearby airstrip, or a boat that was floating a nearby river. They could lure people to the motel with the promise of much more in store.

In the years that followed, the Foushees more than once had to drag their own double bed into a motel room to accommodate guests. "You bite off a whole new set of problems," Gene explains. "You serve the public, and they're your boss, from fixing the pop machines, to renting a room, to unstopping the sewer. Both of you need a combination of talents you didn't ever know you needed. People are always asking us, 'What's your rate of occupancy, what's your return on investment?' We don't even know what our investment *is*."

"It's not that we're counterculture when it comes to money," says Mary. "We like money. But every bit we get goes back into the business in some way."

The great living room of the Foushees' lodge overflows with books and the interesting company of their guests. There's something about the way that light comes into the warm room that explains why quality of life is more important than return on investment.

Recapture Lodge has twenty-one rooms and is near Bluff—a town Mary says is filled with winos and weirdos. Indians stand around posing on street corners (such as they are, a crossing of two paths) as if they were on a movie back lot. Little crumbling adobe buildings make up a main street that would be more comfortable in Spain than in Super Value, Kwik Chek, Hinky Dinky America. And all around wherever you look are the bluffs, great walls of them, red brown and rounded with age—like the country, awesome and comforting, too.

In the cases of the Mitchells, the Grahams, and the Foushees, they picked the place first, then figured out what they were going to do to make money. "If anyone had told me I'd be running an inn and restaurant," Mitchell says, "I'd have told them they were crazy." They had never even *been* to Maine before the weekend they drove up and bought the inn on an impulse. Yet tourism is the obvious business for people who love the land the way they do.

There's a lot of playing it by ear in deciding what to do. There's a lot of adapting, a lot of taking advantage of whatever comes up, saying, "Sure I can do that," without ever having done it before. We have been so shaped by education that we're afraid to attempt things we've not been schooled for. No one could have told the Grahams they would be landlords of a group of condominiums, and surely no one could have convinced Kris that she would move from schoolteacher to bartender. But that's the real freedom of getting out, of doing something by another set of rules—not society's and not yours exactly, but a set of rules made to apply just there, just for you and the time and the work.

Of course you can imagine yourself running a restaurant: It's 7 P.M., the candlelight is burning, the voices are hushed in conversation with an occasional laugh. You circulate quietly among the tables and inquire after the blanquette de veau, the tenderness of the sole. "Marvelous," the guests reward you. "Just great." You answer the phone and take another reservation for four at nine and

you muse that maybe you should try a bit more garlic in
the gigot.

That's running a restaurant? It's funny how we immediately identify with the maître d' instead of the cook, or
the waitress, or the dishwasher. People who get out to run
restaurants have to be, all four. They worry about the
linen service and getting fresh vegetables and keeping the
help in line or even having help at all.

By the time Bob Bentley decided to get out of market
research at BOAC in New York, he had already been to
several cooking schools and had thought about but rejected starting a restaurant in the Caribbean. A couple of
girls who lived beneath Bob and Sonia Bentley and their
two kids on East Eighty-second Street suggested they
have a look at the Southwest. So, merely as a whim, the
Bentleys, with a partner from New York (who's now into
little theater in Albuquerque), went to the Southwest.
Not content with the new and neon civilization of Albuquerque, they ventured north a bit into the Spanish town
of Corrales. A splendid old hacienda, said to have been
built in 1706, was for sale. Bentley and partner swung a
deal, getting the large house by the side of the road, with
its low, sloping porch in front, for about $65,000. Bent-
ley's friend helped in raising capital to buy the building;
it was Bentley's job to run the restaurant and make it
pay.

Bentley is his own chef and is in the kitchen by eleven
each day to marinate some lamb or cut plum tomatoes
for his chilled tomato bouillon or make the fillings for his
cannelloni. About four each day, a woman comes in to
help set up, and Bob takes off for a swim in a nearby pool

and a nap. He returns in the evening to supervise the kitchen and his wife, Sonia, is there ahead of time, acting as hostess. "It's not so easy to keep smiling for six or eight hours at a time," she says, "but I think we have the best restaurant in the state."

"Maybe," Bob says, "but we were nowhere until we got a liquor license, and if Senator Joseph Montoya hadn't come here to dinner and told us to contact his lawyer, we wouldn't have one yet. It's that kind of thing that can make or break a restaurant."

Life is much different for the Bentleys. They don't have to unlock four locks to go out at night anymore; but they rarely go out at night. And certainly not to dinner. The Bentleys have something else, a restaurant to be proud of. It's charming, with an original menu—a restaurant they'd like to go to themselves.

It has been reported in previous chapters how people get out into other service businesses: small-town newspapering, boat chartering, and car renting, into tourist businesses and real estate, but by far the largest number of people get out into shopkeeping—like Fred Lesswing in his hardware store in Maine, and the Wrights in their jewelry shop in New Mexico.

As a shopkeeper in a small town, you have considerations you'd never have anticipated. For example, if there are two grocery stores in town, you'd better make sure you spend half your food budget in each. Goodwill is all. If there's a line of merchandise you're contemplating that would compete with a fellow shopkeeper's, you'd better think twice. If there's a local newspaper, you'd do well to advertise in it, whether it pulls or not. (If you own a newspaper, you've got to shop in *all* of the shops, but that's another story.) If this neighborliness suggests to your townspeople that you are more than a shopkeeper, that's the whole point.

Running an inn or restaurant is small-scale show biz with you as the director. It's your show, your taste, your personality. And you get all the audience feedback. In turn, you feel a responsibility to produce on a more personal level, which is a far cry from the lowest-common-denominator approach of all big business. You can see it in the clothes shopkeepers wear. The aforementioned slim gold ring in the ear of Don Wright in his Cerrillos, New Mexico, shop and studio; Don Madtson, the emigré from Kansas via Palma, Majorca, with his long golden hair and leather pants, wears bracelets in his antique shop in Santa Fe, "a thing I wouldn't have dared in my store in Kansas." Bob Ballard, leaning against great wheels of cheese in his Vermont country store, habitually hooks his thumbs in wide-striped suspenders and often forgets to shave.

Women with a lot of energy and style have traditionally seen the shop as a way to "express themselves," as their men condescendingly put it. The most successful women in shops have put their imprint on the merchandise in a way that gives them the identity they need. It's just this need to express that draws many corporate men into their own stores, where they can bedeck themselves and their windows, chat a lot with their customers, fill a material need in a very personal way, whether it's ski equipment or seventeenth-century English antiques.

Providing a service in a personal way is the most compelling reason most Gotten Out have for doing what they do. But nowhere in the ranks of people in service industries is this point made more clearly than in the case of Jim Hubbard, Virgin Island exterminator.

Jim Hubbard was an engineer and an administrator in his family's successful spring-manufacturing business in Detroit. He is an avid sailor, and when his divorce coincided with an opportunity to deliver a boat to Ecuador with his girl Dee Dee, he didn't even think twice. Through a long tale of sea misfortunes and a tangle with officials on the island of Grenada, Jim and Dee Dee found themselves in St. Thomas with little money and no work. It's hard to imagine this impressively articulate, measured, and moustached man, fresh from the security of a spring factory in Detroit, on St. Thomas without a plan. He says, "When one begins to take oneself too seriously, then there is no place on the island for him. You ask almost invariably, 'If I stay, how can I make a living?' If a person came here [St. Thomas] and he has to ask somebody how to do it, the question comes to mind, Can he make it? Not that you don't need help. If you are a humble person and if you know nobody does it by himself, you can be successful."

At their start, Jim and Dee Dee stayed at the Yacht Haven Hotel, and it wasn't long before they saw the place needed help. They were hired on as managers, but the hotel was in receivership and there was no money for repairs. So they redecorated forty rooms with petty cash, doing the work themselves. During this stint, they became friendly with many of the charter-boat owners out of the marina, and they became acquainted with the scourge of the docks, river rats and cockroaches (which are euphemistically called "palmetto bugs" in the islands). The Hubbards couldn't afford a carpenter at

Yacht Haven, much less an exterminator, so Jim started talking to chemical manufacturers, trying to solve the rodent problem. He came up with some pretty good methods, and soon the charter-boat captains were asking him to derat their yachts. Jim became more intrigued with the possibilities of money in bugs as their stay at Yacht Haven ended. For one thing, the problem existed. Once, as Dee Dee lay on the operating table at the hospital, she saw palmetto bugs dancing overhead on the ceiling near her bed. Also, Jim observed that the native exterminators were wont to go into restaurants and spray dishes as well as flying ants.

Jim had a business friend on the mainland and interested him in investment possibilities. Shortly after, they bought an existing exterminating business on St. Croix and one on St. Thomas. Jim found island-hopping too difficult and the native help on St. Croix hard to manage in transit, so within six months he bought out his partner in the St. Thomas operation and it was all his, "lock, stock, and all its barrels." Jim the exterminator startled some of their chicer friends on the island and offended one rather proper woman, who cried, "Whatever do you want to kill *bugs* for?"

Jim describes the learning experience this way: "The thing you really find out about is yourself: what you can and can't expect. I've been able to build this business slowly by referrals. When I see people who owe me money, I knock on their door and stretch my hand out— a thing that once would have made me crawl inside. But here it's different. You don't make friends by extending credit."

Sure it's strange for an upper-middle-class engineer/intellectual to become an exterminator. But stranger still is the sense of identity and gratification he gets from it. "When I go by someone's house and I see he's having trouble with his foundation, I go in and say, 'Look, Henry, the termites are getting at you rather badly.' And Henry is pleased and grateful. Sometimes I get calls in the middle of the night and it's a customer, frantic: 'Help, there's a mongoose in the bedroom.' And I go down there and take care of it for him and get a great sense of satisfaction from it because he needs me. I probably should have been a country doctor instead of an engineer way back then."

But that was long ago. And now Jim Hubbard finds fulfillment in performing his own service, which he never did playing it the way you're supposed to do it.

10

Money

Now the idea sounds good, the places seem great, even the jobs could be interesting enough—but what about the money? "If only I had the money to do it," you're probably saying to yourself. "It takes money, you know, to get into another business, send kids to school, to live. I simply don't have the money."

That's what you think.

You forget that getting out really is changing your standard of living. Even if you're cutting your income by two-thirds, you're also cutting your obligations, your material goods, your needs, not to mention your taxes. I know. It never seems to you that you're making any money now, so fast does it go out. And what if you had to cut *that* in half? Help! But wait. Look at your fiscal life through the green-colored glasses of a banker, and what do you see? Perhaps you own a house. You just can't assume that house is a series of mortgage payments and nothing else. A house is equity and a convertible asset— eminently legal tender if you change your way of living. Think about your life-insurance policy. Your only contact with it is probably the check for premiums you pay. But the cash value of that insurance can be used as collateral for a loan, or you can borrow back what you've already paid at about 5 percent interest, and you don't lose what you've already paid. Every insurance policy has a handy chart to figure out what it's worth if it's cashed in or borrowed upon.

Then there are the little investments you've made here and there, not doing too well, maybe, but even if you take a loss, there's money there all the same. And what about enforced savings that come out of your company paycheck automatically—retirement plans, pension funds, stock-purchase plans, bonus incentives, and (if you're high enough in the hierarchy) deferred income. With all that going out so regularly and relentlessly, no wonder it seems like you don't have any money. Funds in this nonliquid form seem like solid waste.

But though the money you have "tied up" may seem worthless to you now, you just may be able to run off with a piece of it. It is an ironic commentary on the great corporate world that with all these deferrings and incentives and little investments, they set you up with a pretty good way out of the very company that's paternalizing you.

Then there are the Things. Car payments and credit

cards and revolving charge accounts. Not to mention social life—liquor, entertainment, even clothes and cleaning. When you change your way of living, the money
you've talked yourself into having to spend to live the
way you're used to simply doesn't have to be spent. You
don't get it back. It's not that easy. But instead of trading
your car in every other year and assuring yourself of high
monthly payments, you just hang on to the car until it
won't go any farther. And that may be a long way. Furs,
jewelry, and fine furniture can quickly revert back to
cold hard cash.

When your entertainment is walking in the woods of
an evening, when your bright lights are stars, and your
brass is an occasional crow, it seems all of a sudden that
money spent to see a show, or throw one, is useless and
unnecessary.

It is the normal suburban syndrome to move out of one
rather expensive house and take the equity with you,
plunking it down in still another if larger showplace. Getting out, the process changes. Equity goes into your business, and you consciously opt to live simpler—you can
get a lot more for a lot less Out There. (My husband and
I paid a third less rent a month for a five-room house on
over an acre with barns and a ten-acre pasture than I did
for a studio apartment on Fifty-sixth and Lexington Avenue in New York, and we haven't even gotten out—yet.)

As Mike Mitchell explained when he first saw the
Coveside Inn in Maine, "We said, 'We don't want to buy
that kind of thing.' Then the next thing you knew we
were making an offer on it and we didn't have enough
money. So we went to a local bank and told them what
we had paid for our house in Connecticut and what it

was worth now. And we borrowed—made a short-term loan—against the sale of our house, and that's how we moved. People in suburbia say, 'I don't have any money, I couldn't move.' But they forget they got the house five or ten years ago and they have a lot of equity in it, plus probable appreciation in its market value. We found that the local banks think if you're willing to work, they'll go all the way with you. They're great. They were a tremendous help to us. We have to borrow money each year to get the place open. Hell, we're broke now. We need the money in April to get opened. Last week I was in the bank talking to Walter Chapman and I said, 'Well, Walter, I'll be down about the first of April,' and he said, 'Okay, good, I'll be here.' "

And what about taxes? Granted this system is as inequitable as they come, but one thing is sure: the rage and the helplessness you feel at being unmercifully taxed for precious little gain seems to fade away for the Gotten Out. They no longer feel like prisoners of the state because (1) for the first few years anyway, their own business—be it a homestead or a hardware store or a roadside flower stand—has built-in tax benefits; (2) because their equity is in their work and not in their house, and because of where they got out to, property taxes are minimal; and (3) because their income is of a small and manageable size, they are removed from the strain and tension even the coolest wheeler-dealer feels. Money is yours again even if there's much less of it.

And a strange thing: having less money, by choice, means that you want to buy less. I remember Ea Heuermann, sitting on the deck of the yacht they charter out of St. Thomas, saying, "It's such a great feeling to be looking through magazines or newspapers and see ads for things, you know, all kinds of things and to be able to say to yourself, 'I don't need this or that,' and more important, 'I don't even want it.' We have grown accustomed to the irrational: to stalking the newest and the latest, to hearing that our two-year-old stereo is not worth repairing, and to reasoning that if a television repair costs $50 we're really smarter to spend $350 and get a new one." Once you're out, it's not smugness or self-satisfaction but a reacquaintance with the value of things that makes a difference in needing less, wanting less.

But what if you still don't have enough capital to get out? The first question of course is how much is enough? The Nearings and McCaffreys point out in Chapter 7 that a fall-back-on pool of several thousand dollars is mandatory. This of course goes for small businessmen as well. But if your house equity isn't enough (or you rent) and your corporate benefits are less than substantial, think of this—your present job is collateral. With whom? With the local bank of your prospective small town or county. It's one of those easily mouthed truisms that small towns are drying up, fighting for their lives, losing people to big cities. But small towns almost always have banks. And small-town banks with their small-town bankers are vitally interested in keeping that place quite alive. So, they see a prospective responsible, qualified, currently well-employed citizen wanting to come and set up business in their town, and it's the next best thing to roast beef and biscuits and church on Sunday. Bankers are not usually adventurous, but when they see a big-city executive, they're not going to turn him away easily (for want of capital). Even on the state bank level, in such places as Maine, Wyoming, and New Mexico, there's a great deal of bias toward lending to outside professionals. There has been a state or local bank in back of almost every successful gotten-out business I've visited.

And it's not only banks that want to see you succeed. By reaffirming the business health of a small community, you're pleasing the town's business people. As Miles Turnbull in Monticello, Utah, says, "If at some point the bank were to call their loan on my newspaper, I feel sure I could find a couple of local angels."

Any competent lawyer should know how to get a loan from the federal government's Small Business Administration, whose rules are always changing, but who *have* been known to finance a Gotten Out or two. But small banks are less complicated and a lot better for community relations in a small town.

There are still other ways to set yourself up.

Colby Wilson's Wyoming hostel grew out of a dream in a parking lot. There they were, the whole family—five kids—having made the long drive out from Cleveland in search of a weekly newspaper that in the course of the drive had mysteriously quadrupled in price.

In Cleveland, Wilson worked for a company whose business was selling ink and supplies to newspapers (thus the notion that he wanted one of his own). He was forty-five and the thought of twenty more years until retirement supplying newspapers was "absolutely unbearable."

"Wha'd'ya say, kids," you can almost hear Wilson asking to a carful of children whose ages span more than a decade. "We want to live here," was the unanimous answer. Since all they could see as they sat in the parking lot of the newly hatched Jackson Hole Ski Area were other inns, the Wilsons settled on their own version: "a European hostel with American plumbing." As if the kids could see themselves in their new life of pushing vacuum cleaners and hauling wood. As if Wilson could already see himself in the Marlboro Man image he has since built for himself—ten-gallon perpetually on graying head, rugged features, cowboy boots, and a way of leaning on doorways that John Wayne must have taught him.

So the story goes, they managed to put a hold on the land and find an architect who drew up plans overnight for the sixty-five-unit hotel. Jubilant, the Wilson Seven made their way back to Cleveland, somehow not worrying about the one thing they lacked: money.

Once back in Cleveland, Wilson took the hastily drawn plans to a group of lawyers and drew up the corporation—Hostels, Inc., a company that didn't, in fact, exist. Wilson says, "I took corporate financing in the fifties at the University of Pennsylvania and twenty years later I used the word 'debenture' for the first time." And that was how the stock was sold—thousand-dollar debentures that yield 6 percent interest over a twenty-year period. Wilson sold them to old army buddies, college friends, to his newspaper customers, and lawyers, doctors, and dentists. "Everyone who had ever been West said, 'Here's $1000. Go to Wyoming for me.'"

In all, there were 140 stockholders with one to five shares each. The Wilson family has 57 percent of the stock, which they bought with their equity from the substantial house in suburban Cleveland and the pension accumulated from Wilson's company. "You really can't holler at a system that lets you walk away with this much equity," Wilson says.

Now there really *is* a Hostels, Inc., with franchises starting in Doylestown, Pennsylvania, and Big Sky, Montana. "Every stockholder (most of them friends) comes out to visit his investment, which is great for us because we always see our old friends. And almost every guy who walks in here wonders, 'What could I do to make a living out here?' I tell them all there is the tourist business. Practically everyone who comes out here starves the first few years. You have to have built up some money along the way, because you certainly don't make it here. You just barely make a living, not a fortune. But the good thing is, if you make less than half as much as you did back home, you spend much less too. The first year out here, the lawyers back in Cleveland were angry that I didn't take enough money out of the business to live on. But you just don't spend it here."

The hostel itself is rough-hewn and easy-going inside and out. Walls are unpainted plywood, and just like the ski lodge it is, guests are free to write whatever they like on its walls. Guest rooms are spare and clean with a lot of light wood. "Holiday Inn spends about $10,000 a unit in construction costs," Colby says, "but we spend less than $5000. People are happy when they get here. They do a lot of skiing and use the common rooms in the evening, so these rooms are more than comfortable. All you need in the innkeeping business is to learn how to treat the help like human beings and the guests like friends. We manage without much help, really. It's a ma and pa operation." Ma, Pa, and the kids. The Wilsons' reputation around Jackson Hole is of one big happy family running the hostel like their home.

Buying an existing business may be an easier way of getting out than creating a corporation from scratch. But, though they counsel otherwise, many people have bought businesses that were in doubtful shape. Bob Ballard, of the Weston Village Store says, "People looking to get out should search out a small business that is successfully operating, run by an older couple who may soon want to retire and sell." Sounds good, but as I've pointed out before, Ballard's store was in poor condition when he bought it against the recommendation of his accountant. When Fred Lesswing bought N. G. Marshall Hardware in York, Maine, it had been doing poorly for years. Says Rosemarie Lesswing, "If the business had been successful and the stock in good shape, I don't think Fred would have wanted it. It wouldn't have been enough of a challenge."

But other people's stories sound remote when you can't figure out how to do it yourself. So let's get back to money. More specifically, to *your* money. At the risk of oversimplifying, try this financial analyst's technique of finding out where your strengths (and weaknesses) are. The process of figuring out your net worth is really a first step in getting out. It goes a long way toward separating the dream from the reality. Get a piece of paper and figure it this way:

Assets

LIQUIDS—Money you can get fast. This includes cash

on hand, balances in checking accounts, balances in savings accounts (bank savings and loan or credit union), U.S. Savings Bonds, and cash value of life insurance. Adding these up you get a total of monies whose values never fluctuate, except to go up.

INVESTMENTS—Money you can get pretty fast. These include stocks and bonds, mutual funds, any notes or mortgages owed to you, and whatever pieces of business or action you own. Of course, you may not want to sell these if the market is down, but you can get some money out of them.

EQUITY—Money you forget you have. This includes your home, your second home, and whatever property you own. Your equity is not just the money you have in principal, but based on the market value of these properties, what you're likely to make.

SOLIDS—Things you can sell for less than they're worth. These include things precious and semiprecious, like jewelry and furs and your four-channel stereo and your eight-track tape deck; all the furnishings and small appliances and large appliances; boating equipment and boats; golfing equipment; cars; bicycles; wagons; wheelbarrows; and clothing.

Liabilities (money you don't have)

PAYOFFS—Bills outstanding; charge accounts, credit cards, and other installent payments; medical and dental bills.

MONTHLIES—Auto-loan payment; other loans or debts, personal notes. (Don't figure your house mortgage; you'd be selling that, remember.)

Yearlies—This year's federal, state, and property taxes.

Now add up the liabilities and subtract from your assets (or, God forbid, the other way around) and you should get a pretty good idea of your present financial picture with all the hidden monies exposed. If you're not disheartened, or bored, by this exercise, try making another list. This one of proposed expenses in the new life. Try to assess, at the deflated rates of small towns, what your monthly requirements would be, to assess how much you'd need.

Bare Necessities (by the month)

Housing—a less expensive house, or rental property; utilities; telephone.

Food—remember, fewer dinner parties, and you might grow your own asparagus.

Transportation—Make the old car run, and probably one will do. You live almost at your place of business, so no commuting. Recreation is at hand. No need to fly or drive long distances.

Doctor Bills—You may not need medical help less, but routine bills are much less expensive out of the specialized big city. Medical insurance.

Savings and Investment—Life insurance, education for children, uninsured emergencies. Either a rather large nest egg, or confirmed borrowing power.

Clothing and Maintenance—You don't have to buy much but you do have to clean it.

If you can approximate numbers for the preceding categories, you can get a very rough idea of how your daily and monthly living expenses change with getting out. You may be surprised how little you can get by on. It may make you confident that you can, in fact, cut your income and still provide.

II

Alternate Wife-Styles

The women of my generation were not prepared for life. The realities of existence were not part of our training and education. We're not equipped to function in the lives we live.
Frances Kaufman in *The New York Times*, February 7, 1972

Of course, it is not just the man's decision to chuck his title and get out. Looking at the corporate family as it exists today, it is obvious that the wife is in real trouble. As a mother and housekeeper she is purveyor of punishments. She is as a child to new and inventive ideas brought home by the father/husband, with too much resentment to learn easily and not enough time to perfect interests of her own. Eagerness to know how a washing machine works is easily dispelled by the frustration of not having it working. It is perhaps the greatest irony that she stays home to take care of and raise her children only to be mistaken by her husband for one of them.

But no matter how undesirable the role of wife in the seventies, what is a woman of thirty-five, or thirty-eight, or forty-two, or forty-six to do? The Movement hasn't successfully answered the need of liberation these women have. It is far easier for the young to revolt; they are free and need give up only ideas—not children, not husbands, not safe homes. What can the wife do with youthful skills lost or forgotten, with a shaky notion of her ability to cope with what is to her the outside world?

Women's magazines publish endless housewife-extolling articles that show how the hapless hausfrau in her workaday drudgery is really the Doris Day paradigm of success: "Why," they breathlessly write, "think of this, you are really an administrator, a purchasing agent, a dietitian, interior decorator, a personnel manager, a public relations director." All I can say about that is just try to get her a job as one of them.

Besides lacking skills, she is indentured and obligated. How could she *refuse* to spend her days cooking or cleaning or doing the laundry? Her husband works so hard. He is making the money she spends—she lives on— how could she not fill her part of the bargain?

Put this way, it's not the wife, but the bargain that's wrong. A social contract that calls for a man to be automatically and solely responsible for making the money, to bear alone the burden of producing, while the wife, by default, is mistress of all the dreary rest—this contract is as inequitable and debilitating as the society that wrote it. If getting out is the way for a man to exchange his own rules for those of his company, getting out is a way for a woman to find real equality the second time around. When a husband and wife decide on a business together, the wife can—by working at it shoulder to shoulder and hand in hand—find her own identity.

For the wife, getting out is her husband's commitment to her as well as to himself. By saying "my career no longer comes first," he means that the everyday quality of his life does come first. No more long-distance calls, "Staying in town, dear," no more summer bachelorhood.

With this new sharing, the husband doesn't go "off to work" any more than the wife does, because whatever they undertake to do, it just isn't enough to have one person working at it. And because the business, be it restaurant, inn, shop, newspaper, is a beginning for him as well, they begin together. She need have for previous experience only her boundless energy and her willingness to make a go of it. This purposely simpler way of earning a living doesn't have any occupational mystique about it. Innate intelligence, not a résumé, is required.

Household and work place become integrated without a rigorous suburban chauffeuring of kids to friends and lessons. Kids know the store, for instance, as well as their suburban family room, and probably spend more inventive time there, making it a real family room. With her new importance to her business, a wife is able to be her own person. There is no need for her social graces to polish up her husband's good name. Dinner parties? Family dinners just happen at the end of days spent working together, cooking together.

Roles blur around the edges and gradually dissolve.

Does this sound like those everyone-lived-happily-ever-after stories? It's not. I can think of over a dozen women who changed their lives this way—by getting out with their husbands. Most of these wives were not working when their families got out.

Mary Foushee of Recapture Lodge in Bluff, Utah, says, "I cried for about six months before we left Union Carbide. I would wake up in the middle of the night with a feeling of impending doom. Even though I looked around me and saw that all the other corporate wives seemed to adjust better and play bridge and be good women voters, and I knew I was never too good at that, I was still scared. Now I can't imagine staying home as a housewife. I think for a successful marriage you need a common goal—a good partnership." Mary had been an executive secretary before she left to marry Gene and have their daughter.

On the masthead of the *San Juan Record*, Jane Turnbull's name is right up there next to Miles's as publisher. Says Miles, "The most important thing is that we're together. We scream at each other, things go wrong, but it's good to be working together. I wouldn't recommend this, however, to a couple who's having any trouble." Jane was writing ad copy when she met Miles and stopped working to have her family. It was about seven years till they got out.

For a woman, getting out is the ultimate-risk partnership. If you're really good together, you'll be great together, but if your lives were really separate and being married was just a convenience, starting a new life will point that up. In St. Thomas, which is traditionally a divorce mill, many couples who came to the island ten years ago just aren't together anymore. It is a personal confrontation, where couples ill-met no longer have separate lives to retreat into.

Jacques Ellison, public relations man for the Virgin Islands in St. Thomas and a sympathetic, well-known, local television figure, had this sad story to tell: "When we first got here, I found newspaper work and advertising work that really turned me on. Barbie was in library science, and she found library work here impossible. We're just now developing some good libraries on the island. Our marriage ran into trouble. It happened to us as it does to many couples on the island. She couldn't stay and I couldn't leave."

Bill and Ea Heuermann say they've seen many couples try to run away from all their problems on a boat. Inevitably, one stays and one goes. Ea says, "You have to be madly in love with someone to stand it on a boat. Otherwise, you'll kill him. Very slowly, but kill him." So far everything is peaceful aboard the *Jupiter*. Ea is a galley cook for other people on their vacations, and she couldn't be happier if she still had someone cooking for her.

Rosemarie Lesswing has never worked in the thirteen years she has been married to Fred; she was too busy moving eleven times and having four children. Now newly settled in York, Maine, she does all the advertising and works on the books for the N. G. Marshall hardware store and is studying for a real estate broker's license. "It's great to be able to work together—it's saying 'we' instead of 'I'."

Kid-Styles

Concern for her children can keep a woman from getting out. There's no question that the children have always belonged to her. She was the one to use her own education for the sole purposes of bringing them up; she the Florence Nightgown, she the martyr and sacrificer of her own needs and pleasures. And where has it gotten her? Or them? Being the vicarious-living vessels, Mama's

Baby, has psychologically maimed enough otherwise charming young men (and women) to provide the wherewithal for hundreds of shrinks to spend the entire month of August on Martha's Vineyard.

The mother is the crusader for good schools, but the middle-class school system has become plain and simple an extension of the corporate mentality, an amplification of the husband's job and the roles he sets up for himself. (That's at its stifling best, for the suburban school life has bred a physical destruction more immediate and more perverse.) Getting out can be a real solution. There is an old-time spirit about small-town schools that preserves a child's identity.

Mike Mitchell talks about the problems of a child in suburbia: "When you live in Darien, or Scarsdale, from the moment a child is out of school in the afternoon, it's a thing with parents to have a planned day until the time they go to bed. So you go to a Cub Scout meeting in Darien, Connecticut, and it isn't the little boys making their racing cars, it's a competition with their daddies to see who can make the fastest one. I know, I used to do it in our basement workshop. The Little League is something to see. You can't tell me the daddies aren't pushing harder than the kids.

"The epitome of the school attitude is a guy I met at a cocktail party one night in Darien. I'll never forget it. He said to me, 'Do you have a six year old?' And I said, 'Yes.' And he said, 'You ought to have him tested— there's a great place in Norwalk.' And I said, 'What does that do?' 'Well, they'll tell you where he's weak and where he's strong.' And I said, 'Then what happens?' He said, 'Well they'll sum that up and he'll get into a good prep school.' And I said, 'Then what happens?' He said, 'Then he'll get into a good college.' And I said, 'Then what happens?' 'Well,' the guy said, 'then he'll get a good job.' And I said, 'And be a snob like you?' "

There's no need to indulge in long and lurid tales of kids and grass and kids and dope to tell what happened to the middle-class school system. It was this attitude of succeeding, of doing the prescribed thing, that perpetuated the breakdown from within. Clearly it was not enough to get a lot of bright kids from comfortable families and put them in a school where they'd be given the right college-prep courses. This was no challenge for Have-nots, it was an internecine rumble of the Have-mores and the Have-still-more-than-thats.

It may be too easy to blame the corporate mentality for the breakdown of the suburban dream, but something has certainly gone wrong. The criteria are topsy-turvy and the superior living conditions once sought after suddenly don't look like that at all. Carolyn McClean, who moved with her husband, Dugald, from Omaha, Nebraska, to Sydney, Australia, says it: "It was a definite advantage for our children to move out of an upper-middle-class, WASPish ghetto community into the more cosmopolitan, more mixed city of Sydney. We live in a working section, and the kids have gone to state schools and I think sampled life in a much more real way than they would have in the situation we lived in in the U.S."

Parents are finding out that responsibility and security are no longer by-products of the safe and sure middle class. Many parents feel they have to get out in order to really let their kids develop as individuals: to help them find out who they are and not turn them into who they

should be. It can be argued that kids like the Mitchells'
son, who runs a boat dock at fifteen, are succumbing to
the meaningless work ethic their fathers have rejected—
the old-time rules of discipline and responsibility. But
parents who have gotten out feel this strongly—children
are told that the success of the family's life in this new
place is very dependent on their ability to help. Children
are needed, appreciated, respected, and, oh yes, paid.

It's hard to observe sets of children for a day or two
and then automatically conclude that the sins and excesses of suburbia have been purged. Most of the parents
seem to think they have been. Teenagers grow, work, assume responsibility (instead of the family car), and in
general rid themselves of the materialism the whole family found itself in.

The younger gotten-out child has a bit of the Tom
Sawyer in him and can fool around by himself in in-
tensely personal ways. Barbara Wright of Cerrillos, New
Mexico, says of her kids, "There are no ballet lessons—
that's true. But the kids can take off and go camping in
the hills anytime they want. Unlike the city, where all
our friends thought the same and dressed the same, in
New Mexico they have a three-culture experience that
has a great deal to teach them. The only thing they have
to watch out for is snakes in the arroyo."

Jane Turnbull says their young boy and girl are in and
out of the newspaper office all the time. "We can teach
them how to run a newspaper. They already know a lot.
And it's a great feeling that we have this to teach them."

I've observed that the families I've met are truly families, not a collection of semistrangers passing in a hostile
and very lonely night, on the way to some activity. The

five Wilson kids are as involved in the hostel as their parents. People who stay there say it's like being guests of one big family; the six Lesswings bicycle together on hardware store inventory every Sunday; the Mitchells' kids help run the Coveside Inn.

Obviously getting out is not a panacea. But there are examples of fractured families getting back together with a common goal, parent and parent, and parent and child.

Getting the kids out does mean leaving the expensive machinery of suburban school systems—sophisticated science labs and audio-visual equipment. It may also mean that in the new surroundings the English teacher is also the football coach, or that there's nobody around to teach Latin. These are very real concerns in the getting-into-college mentality of present educational systems. (But with current geographical quotas, a bright kid from Maine probably has a much better chance of getting into Harvard than a kid from New York any day.)

But it doesn't mean that there aren't good school systems in the sticks. Many teachers get out and still teach. The little town of Jackson, Wyoming, for example, attracts so many teachers that even on the elementary level, many have Ph.D.'s. When I was a little skeptical about the school system, one Jackson resident said there were six hundred applicants for eleven jobs last year. Further, he went on to extol the merits of their new principal, who turned out, with weird coincidence, to have been my own eighth-grade teacher back in Westport, Connecticut.

Not only do teachers get out and still teach but doctors get out and still practice medicine—an encouraging thing when you're far from civilization. The fact is that many dentists, lab technicians, lawyers, college professors, and nurses have gotten out and, in practicing their skills, have made the places they move to better for the others who live there.

12

Second Thoughts and Paranoia

To people whose way of life is being in touch, the prospect of being out of it is frightening. I know. Just two
years ago, midst the raging of the skirt-length contro-
versy, I left New York. I had hardly gotten out. I had
gotten married. I was working harder than ever, but I
moved to Des Moines, Iowa, less chic than which one
cannot get. And the questions began to do me in: "How
are you going to work out there?" "Don't you feel out of
touch?" Although my ready answer was something like,
"You carry your culture on your back," I was really par-
anoid about it. The first time I went back to the city was
after about six weeks. I got into a cab at La Guardia with

several other people. I was audibly annoyed that the cab-
bie was "taking us!" and right away began to ask the
driver why he was going Northern Boulevard instead of
the Hoyt Avenue exit off the Grand Central Parkway. I
was even a little ashamed to have to give my destination
in front of everyone as a hotel, not an apartment (but at
least it *was* the Algonquin). I kept thinking—as if I were
back in Paris trying to pass—does the driver really think
I'm still a New Yorker?

Most New Yorkers don't. One friend of mine never
fails to put bitter little doubts in me. "How do you know
what's going on out there? Don't you feel out of it?"

"Oh," I answer breezily, "they've got newspapers out
there. And television. They have a lot of television."

"Yeah, but how do you know what's really happening?"

"My phone," I say a little defensively, "has been
known to ring from time to time. And even I pick it up
for a buck and call a friend."

"Yeah, but I think you get out of touch. I mean like
these people who live near us in the country where we
rent a summer house. He's a really bright man, but he
just doesn't care what's going on."

"What do you mean?"

"Well, not long after the Pentagon Papers were
printed in the *Times*, we got this story from our lawyer
that when Punch Sulzberger and Scotty Reston were told
by their legal department that they could possibly go to
jail for printing the papers, Scotty said, 'I'll take that
chance.' And Punch said, 'I won't.' And I thought that
was so interesting. But when we went to see these friends

who live near us in the country and we told them that story, they really weren't interested at all. I mean he reads the *Times* and everything. But he's just out of touch."

Now these kinds of stories have a way of working on me, even if I don't care about the substance at all. Even your best friends, it turns out, will not spare you the surge of insecurity that comes from, "Oh, you wouldn't know about that, you're from Des Moines." In the beginning I retaliated with, "Well, if I'd been in Paris for six weeks you wouldn't think I was out of it. Just imagine I live in Paris," which of course didn't work.

My last self-defensive resort was to start keeping a notebook of things people said to me about being out of touch. You see, ostensibly I was secretly collecting material that I would *use* later on, and that higher purpose would soothe the bitter wounds inflicted by the verbal abuse of the near, the dear, and the mean.

Note: On the phone to a New York graphic designer, I got off an admittedly bad pun. "You come to New York, we'll sharpen you up," he said.

Note: In a restaurant in New York with an old friend. "Well," he said, "I'm glad to see you can still order in a French restaurant."

Note: In meeting an old friend on Lexington Avenue. "And that's a Des Moines dress you're wearing," she observed. I had bought it minutes before at Bloomingdale's.

Note: After three months "out of it" a childhood friend said, "You're starting to talk different. You have a Midwestern accent." Searching through the dozens of people I work with in Des Moines, I realized that everybody comes from somewhere else and that I knew only one real-honest-to-goodness Iowa boy I could have learned Midwestern from, and he's a poet.

Note: "You've been in Des Moines too long," said a friend when I shook his outstretched hand instead of slapping him some skin.

I have gotten out in address only. My feelings, though, are typical of the doubts and fears people have who have just made the decision to get out and don't have the comfort of a successful new life-style to back them up.

An ex-Playboy Bunny from New York said she was petrified to get out to New Mexico with her new husband. "My great fear," she told us, "was that there would be no people around. There are only a million people in the state, and I had that many in my apartment building."

Another young woman, newly moved with her husband to New Mexico, has *The New York Times* mailed to her, and when it comes, four days late, she gobbles it up, as if it weren't at all like reading yesterday's newspaper. She also gets a care package from Zabar's, that munificent store on New York's Broadway, of coffee (special grind), Brie cheese, well-wrapped Nova Scotia salmon, and several large dill pickles. Sitting in her living room, you can hear the low tones of a tape—Larry Josephson, disc jockey/raconteur for New York's listener-sponsored radio station, WBAI. It's on almost all the time, soon the words blur to a reassuring New York hum—the comfort of urbane Muzak out there on the mesa.

Though the fear of being out of touch is very real, in reality it is a nineteenth-century fear imposed upon a twentieth-century world. Back when people were born, lived, and died in the same small town, there was a huge difference between town life and that in the city. It was a difference of mentality as well as of mobility. One did not leave the small town. To be sure, there was no easy way out, but they didn't leave because it simply was not done. The rules of local church and school and mama and papa were life-rules There were no alternatives; none were allowed. People who get out to small towns today are not just only as far away as the nearest airport. They are free to go. And come. Mobility is as natural to our way of life as the telephone. These factors have all but eliminated the notion of provincialism, and the urban sophisticated should understand this.

Big-city people—even the Mediamakers themselves— far underestimate the pervasiveness of mass communication in this country. Attitudes and catchphrases thought up in a brainstorming session over delicatessen sandwiches soon come out whole over radio, TV, and magazines into kitchens of the smallest towns, where beans and greens or tacos or eggs-over-easy are cooking. The United States is just a market, a military map for the McDonalds of the world to plan their franchised strategies. It is the marketing managers of information and products that really disseminate culture in our society. The same top-ten songs are played from Maui, Hawaii, to Bar Harbor, Maine. The high-pitched scream of self-adulation heard on talk shows is often far too available to even the remotest antenna. The issues and concerns of America are there for the listening. The same jabbers and chatters that clutter up the night sky can be tuned in anywhere on this continent. The products the media tout are only as far as the corner store, general or not. The question becomes, then, "Why keep in touch?" and not "Don't you feel out of it?" The question is rather, "Where can you find regional individuality?" And the quest is for some place far away from mass communication.

Getting out means getting away from the whole wash of information and communication that has been a constant bombardment on the brain for years. It is almost like a debriefing of everything you're supposed to know in the real world, than a selective policy about what is going to be readmitted.

Once out, you get to the point where a lot of things just don't make a difference. One of the funniest examples of this was in a letter from Bill Heuermann, ex-San Francisco investment counselor, written from the yacht *Jupiter*: "Recently had a day charter with Danny Hutton, singer with Three Dog Night. To show you how out of it we are, we had never heard of the group and I kept calling it Three Night Dog or Night Dog Three, endearing ourselves to Danny, I'm sure."

People in Jackson Hole, Wyoming, spend a lot of time at cocktail parties talking about national issues, to be sure. But they probably spend more time talking about who's running for sheriff and the local legislature, because often it's one of them. Bob Graham says, "You get far more involved with local politics and local news. But it's always inside news and you can deal with it directly. There's an undertone of well-being here. People aren't always worrying about some crushing problem they can't do anything about."

"Americans gotten out to faraway Australia," Immigration Attaché Lionel Mead reports from Washington, "eventually forget about *The New York Times*, if," he adds, "anyone can really ever forget about the *Times*." There are over 600 newspapers for Australia's 12 million people, so one hardly has the sense of a news blackout.

And what about friends? When people tighten up in fear of being forever estranged from those they love, they are again thinking in the nineteenth century. Bob Ballard, owner of the Weston Village Store in Weston, Vermont, says, "The first year we got out, we succumbed to the temptation to rent a big old New England country house. It was a huge mistake. We had guests forty-eight out of fifty-two weekends. At first it was great. You want to show your friends you can still live it up like the old days. You want to demonstrate how great it is to be living here. Then you begin to realize you don't need to live it up, you don't have to unwind like they do. And you can't afford the liquor bills.

"So we moved to a tiny house with no guest room, to sort of discourage the weekend traffic. But the friends we want to see still come up and they stay in town and it works out just fine. Some even take summer houses up here."

Friends are mobile, too. More than that, they're curious. They want to come peek in at the way you're living. They want to measure themselves against what you're doing and see if they could ever do it, too. And another thing, the Gotten Out go to this country's most beautiful places: the mountains, the shore, the sandy Southwest. And friends and family still get the corporate world's

three- or four-week vacation. You become the reason to
go where you are.

You Can Take It with You

Atlantic City, Wyoming, population about 25, is a
long way from anywhere. Last winter, with snowdrifts up
to 20 and 30 feet and an accumulation of 54 inches, resi-
dents of the historic gold-rush town on the old Oregon
Trail didn't go out for weeks. Their food supply was in
Lander, 30 miles away, and the snow kept blowing over
the only road as soon as the highway machinery opened
it.

It was not exactly the life that Paul and Gina Newman
would have chosen for themselves ten years ago. In the
early 1960s, Paul was vice-president of the Cudner Advertising Agency and, with an apartment in New York
and one in Detroit, was responsible for the Pontiac account. Gina was, in those days, an editor on *Living for
Young Homemakers*, a magazine of interiors and furnishings.

The bright and cosmopolitan noise of high life and fast
business followed the Newmans from the East Sixties to
Bloomfield Hills and back again. But all of a sudden it
began to show. *Living*, on shaky financial ground, crum-
bled and merged into an insignificant corner of *House and
Garden*. And Paul developed high blood pressure and was
ordered by his doctor to take a sabbatical. Gina and Paul
resigned themselves to a year of winding down in Mexico
somewhere, and in early 1963 set out for a leisurely trip
across country on their way south.

They knew about Carpenter's Hotel in Atlantic City, Wyoming, from fishing trips years ago, when they'd escape from the big time and fish the swift Sweetwater River that parallels the Oregon Trail. Gina remembered well the days when "Miss Ellen" Carpenter ran the hotel and restaurant like a lodge for the aristocracy in the German Black Forest. There would be elegant dinners of antelope and fresh-caught trout, dispatched with efficiency, as if the hotel were still the only stagecoach stop between Rock Springs and Lander. It was probably nostalgia that brought the Newmans through Atlantic City on their way to Mexico. Nostalgia and good fishing. Little did they know that Miss Ellen Carpenter had died and that Carpenter's Hotel was up for sale. Paul thought it would be amusing to make a bid on the property. Gina thought it was probably safe because they were one of a dozen bidders and the chance they'd get it was slight. So slight that they made their bid and moved on to Mexico.

Not long after that, the letter came. Gina and Paul Newman were the proud new owners of Carpenter's Hotel in Atlantic City, Wyoming, population, at that time, one seventy-eight-year-old man. Somewhat reluctantly, the Newmans returned north to accept their claim, wondering what they would do with it. Gina saw it as a vacation lodge where they could spend several weeks a year. But Paul had other ideas. "Even if my blood pressure is down," he declared, "I am not going back East."

It took Gina a while to fully understand. "Not going back? Not ever going back to New York?" Gina says she became so hysterical that she went into some tavern in Lander and Paul had to get the sheriff to find her three days later.

Paul said, "I had to get out of the ad business. I would have been in a wheelchair in a year."

For Paul the decision had come swiftly and logically— it was probably a matter of life or death. For Gina it was not so simple—it was no longer a matter of "Living." But she was sure, with the deadly certainty New Yorkers feed upon, that she would die in soul, if not in body, if she were to stay. She needed the people, the pace, the noise of the big city. She needed her self-importance and her career. Still, she kept reminding herself, she loved Paul, and as the hysteria ebbed away she reasoned that maybe she could make it if they had a project—a financial as well as an emotional necessity. Back in the New York days, both Paul and she had taken gourmet cooking courses from the biggies, James Beard, Dione Lucas. That was it— they could open a restaurant. Because they didn't want many overnight sleepers, they changed the name to Miner's Delight, after the defunct old gold mine in nearby South Pass, and got a liquor license.

The people from Riverton and Lander said that it couldn't be done. Gina said they warned repeatedly, "These are meat and potatoes folk. They'll never go for a high-falutin' gourmet restaurant they have to drive thirty miles to." But they were wrong. They didn't count on the snob appeal a restaurant run by New Yorkers would have in Wyoming. People in Wyoming may have a cowboy image, but they also have a lot of money, made from cattle, oil, sheep, and smart real estate. Some even have private airplanes. But what they didn't have was culture—fine French cooking.

When I first spoke to Gina Newman, it was long distance from Cheyenne. "Look," I told her, "if we left today we could be in Atlantic City Friday and have dinner and interview you."

"Oh no," she said curtly. "Friday we're having a luau here for thirty-five people and I couldn't possibly fit you in. And we'll be too busy getting ready for another luau Saturday night. But if you get here for the Saturday dinner, maybe we could talk to you after that." We rearranged three days of interviews and planned to get there Saturday.

When I first saw Gina Newman I was walking into her kitchen through the back door just before dinner, and she looked up from a tray of hors d'oeuvres and said, "Oh no, you can't come in here, I'll see you later."

I couldn't believe it. I looked outside to see if maybe we were on East Fifty-seventh Street by mistake. But no, there was the long and dusty gravel road we had traveled forty-five minutes from Lander to see this woman. And she was New Yorking me out of her kitchen. I was thinking, "Look, lady, it took us two days to get here," but there was little else to do but back off and observe how Gina and Paul run a luau. Paul is gray-haired—a thick mane of it—and impressive-looking. He has aged like every man hopes to, which is to say imperceptibly. Tanned, at ease, he has the relaxed bonhomie of many executives in their sixties, and there's nothing that tells he runs a restaurant, not a corporation. He was now in straw hat and aloha shirt, kissing each girl as he put a lei around her neck.

Rising up from the barren, sandy ground around the deck at the back of the restaurant are hills scrubby with

low, wind-twisted trees. You can see for miles—a little
one-room church with a cross silhouetted against the evening sky. Lone shanty buildings with as much age and
character as an old sourdough's face, remain standing
somehow, abandoned. You can see how the road winds
up the sandy hills past the only store in town, the Atlantic City Mercantile Company, where you can buy a little
gas and a little food. And the music. Slack string guitar,
aloha-o-ing into the open air. An old portable record
player was playing Hawaiian music on the back of a
pickup truck, its wire running fifteen feet to a plug inside
the house. What's more, there were pails of live gladioli
sitting everywhere. And cocoanuts and large seashells.
The Newmans were having a luau, right here in turn-of-
the-century Atlantic City, Wyoming.

And Gina came out. Marvelous stage presence. She
sensed the arrival of guests and with arms outstretched,
orchestrated their movements. It's hard to determine her
age, so lithe are the gestures of her slim body in white
pants and tunic. Her dark hair is pulled back tight; her
eyes sparkle and flash over high cheekbones, generously
rouged. She floats leis around the necks of arriving men
and is girlish and cute—neither seems out of place.

Gina is the hostess for this luau, for which every couple
is paying thirteen dollars plus liquor. Some have driven
miles from the surrounding towns, some have flown in
from as far as Casper and Rock Spring. They have come
to hear Gina, in the tones of every cocktail party hostess
on Park Avenue, introduce people to each other not by
who they are but by what they do. "This is our new
young doctor and his wife," she says. "This is an organ-
izer of the National Outdoor Leadership School in Lan-

der. This woman has sponsored little theater in our area. This couple has set up libraries."

"The first *mai tai* is on the house," her throaty, show-biz voice rang out on the deck, which was by now very crowded with people eating appetizers of barbecued pork from smoky grills. There were girls in long print dresses, a few aloha shirts, and older blue-haired but statuesque women with sweaters thrown across their bare shoulders. Cashmere. "You see what kind of crowd we get," Gina says. "No cowboys with hats," she laughed, then moved off to another group. It was a beautiful party, and as the deepest laugh of all floated off, you realize with what professional seriousness Gina and Paul Newman run their business. They treat their guests as friends. They *are* friends, after all. But they *are* guests.

Gradually the group, about thirty in all, moved inside to several tables in the small dining room. The tables were laden and glowing, draped with cloths, set with crystal and silver. Orchids, excusably plastic, were at every lady's plate.

Gina had carefully seated everyone with place cards; there was no confusion. And as she and Paul and a neighbor friend served the four-course luau dinner with grace and some kidding, I found that most of the people had been here many times before. It is their treat of a weekend, and they are *grateful* to the sophisticated New-mans for making their home in Wyoming.

Later, after all the guests have departed, we sat in the kitchen with Gina and Paul as they did the dishes and talked. And the thought struck me here as it did on the deck outside, as it did in their upstairs sitting room with white formal sofas precisely set with stuffed pillows, and polished tables bedecked with carefully chosen *objets,* that the Newmans have indeed gotten out. But they have brought it all with them. They may be out of it, but they are admired and respected for their years of being in.

Paul was saying in the kitchen how in her early career days Gina was the kind of cook who made tuna-noodle casserole from the back of cornflakes boxes and sauces from Campbell's cream of mushroom soup. He, it seems, was the inspiration for gourmet cooking, and he describes in the sanctimonious tones of a missionary how it was getting Wyoming people to eat their first snails. Menus are never a problem for the Newmans because they serve only one appetizer and one entrée and guests love not knowing what they're having to eat. "It's just like going to someone's house for dinner," they say. "You never know what they're going to serve."

Gina and Paul have run Miner's Delight for nine years now, and during the season they still can't take a weekend off for fishing. "If we don't answer the phone, people will think we're closed up." Their season starts about May 1 and runs as far into fall as the roads are negotiable. Most guests call ahead for reservations, so there's always plenty of time to plan. A few bedrooms upstairs, furnished with painted iron bedsteads, are rented out to special guests who have come a long way. The little bar is hung with pictures of the Newmans with famous people, Gina as a model-type young girl. ("Oh I was gor–geous then, all skin and bones.") In the hall you pass a framed copy of *Scribner's* magazine with Paul looking like a young Gatsby on the cover.

Winters, if they get out in time, the Newmans close up and head for a skiing resort where they do the cooking in return for free skiing and board. Steamboat, Park City, Alta, Grand Tarhee, Jackson Hole, they hit them all, often ending up with a few weeks in the South. "This year it was Palm Beach instead of Paris. We had to install a whole new water system."

Atlantic City, Wyoming, has changed since the Newmans took over Carpenter's. Land that had been selling for $150 an acre is suddenly $500. U.S. Steel is bringing miners again into the old mining town, but their gold is iron ore. With the new neighbors have come problems the Newmans don't have with their restaurant friends. "In New York," Gina says, "if you found someone with whom you weren't *simpático,* you found someone else with whom you were. But here, there's no one else." Neighbors, even in a tiny town, can get to be a problem. Like the woman over the hill who resents the Newmans' steady flow of interesting people in and out of their house. "She doesn't realize we're working our fingers to the bone for the business. On top of that, she fancied herself an artist and made the mistake of asking Paul what he *really* thought of her work. He made the mistake of really telling her.

"Once the season is over and work ends, a great deal of your mental stimulation ends," says Gina, whose work is clearly play and whose play is maybe only work. "Paul is a fanatic reader. He can go through fifteen books in two weeks. I can't stand it. In winter, day after day Paul sits and reads, reads, reads, reads."

"That, my dear, is what I'm here for." Paul reminds her once again of what she's already heard a thousand times. Paul is clearly glad to have the other life behind him. "It was losing its excitement," he says. "The crea-

tive man in print media has been stamped out by this
monster television. The fun has gone out of the business."
But not for Gina. She searches for names, now half-for-
gotten, of people she once knew. And here, in her beauti-
fully designed kitchen, this legion of half-familiar faces
become some of the most important in the world because
they each hold a bit of the career woman she once was.
In the big time.

Gina, like a lot of successful women in business, needs
to be a star, and she is one at Miner's Delight. To her pa-
trons, the restaurant is "21" and Sardi's and The Forum
of the Twelve Caesars wrapped into one. But it's better
still than that, because it's *not* in New York. It's here, at
home, in Big Wyoming, which makes it better. Being a
New Yorker was always of paramount importance to
Gina Newman, but she found that she didn't have to stay
in New York for it, and that she was sought after and admired by chauvinistic Wyomingites who would far rather
see than be one.

13

What If You Fail?

Nathaniel Hawthorne, again, in *The Blithedale Romance*, on the verge of getting out of Boston:

> The greatest obstacle to being heroic is the doubt whether one may not be going to prove one's self a fool; the truest heroism is to resist the doubt; and the profoundest wisdom to know when it ought to be resisted, and when to be obeyed.
>
> . . . Whatever else I may repent of, therefore, let it be reckoned neither among my sins nor follies that I once had faith and force enough to form generous hopes of the world's destiny. . . .

If you've had faith and force enough to try, it doesn't really matter if the particular solution works or not. Going back should always be a possible and not at all dishonorable alternative. The wisest and the surest of the Gotten Out have kept the exit ways from their former lives in excellent repair; they have not raised a defiant fist at the system and brought it down irreparably on the only bridge back. There is great temptation, once the real insight into the newer life is found, to repudiate and condemn the old as if the new would be all the brighter for remorse and bitterness. There's the self-righteous inclination to amble downtown to the busiest business thoroughfare, dressed in blue jeans or worse, and loudly revile the sheeplike herds of tied and jacketed employees on their way to be ground up in the system. There's the impulse to preach salvation, or at least hand out mimeographed leaflets: "Quick, Brothers, Before the World Ends, Get Out." But public ranting about your latest acquisition—the holy grail—means that you set yourself up. Any retrenchment or change of plans leaves you open for moral incrimination. A few words suffice: "Don't burn bridges."

Many of the ex-successful businessmen I've interviewed have been enthusiastic in their praise of the old life, bosses, the game. They were careful to leave the system with consummate corporate grace. Many of their old business pals come up to peek in on their new life, and the Gotten Out seem to revel in the attention. I suspect they leave a crack in the office door—just another option. A comfort that, in most cases, soon atrophies for lack of need.

Leaving a crack doesn't mean, of course, withholding

commitment to a new life; it doesn't mean going to the country with one foot still under the desk. It means only to be easy on yourself. To be sure, but not cocky.

Fear of failure, as the psychologists call it, is a powerful deterrent to doing it—it's a powerful deterrent to living at all. All life's moves are only trials, though they're advertised as more. It's been said, but I do believe "it's better to have . . . than never to have. . . ."

To retreat from the abstract, let's look at what the fears really are. Making enough money? We've pretty much shown that though you'll probably earn less, you'll need much less than that. Not liking the work? Real enough, but the work will be what you make it—that was the whole point, remember? Not making any friends. (What if there's no one to talk to?) A lot of that depends on where you go, and usually if you've spent some time in your chosen place checking out businesses, banks, places to live, you've met enough townspeople to get a pretty good idea if you'll ever have anything more to say to them.

Also, the local folk will be quick to tell you about and/or introduce you to people in the area who've done what you're contemplating. And an interview with them is a great way to tell if you're going to like it, or them. The real, most pernicious fear may be as nameless as a little bit of all of the preceding. It's scary to move on in life and probably scarier to build with the possibility of moving back.

You can imagine the scenario: telling your friends and enduring their sometimes disapproving responses; suffering through the going-away parties, which are sustained anticlimax. Then you remain stalwart and uncomplaining through the early, uncertain, and maybe rough first months, all the while feeling *their* scrutinizing eyes searching for a crack in your resolve. (Seeing you falter would, by implication, affirm that *they're* doing it right, after all.) Seeing yourself through *their* eyes can keep you from doing it at all. But getting away from *their* ideas is what getting out is all about.

All of which is *not* to say that you can't fail at getting out. You just simply might not like it. But remember that the discontent and uneasiness and pressure that led you to try would not allow you to slip back in unmarked and unchanged. Having simplified your life enough to make the attempt at all is a huge step in sorting out what's important and what's not. Even if you go back to mainstream society, there is no way to retreat into the same wretched excesses after you've recognized them enough to reject them once.

Maybe you want to go to the movies more than the barn. And maybe you need traffic noises so you can sleep. Perhaps you can't function without the structure of your old ways. And maybe twentieth-century man was bred for the urban, corporate life after all. Okay. So you fail. What have you lost?

Halfway Houses

There are other reasons besides stark fear that keep people from getting out all the way. For years the second home has been the interim solution to getting out and staying in at the same time.

It's not the casual two-hour drive that it used to be to

the house at the shore or in the mountains. The trip has become a highly charged psychological leap between the supremely complex and the sublimely simple, a leap that means, among other things, a lot more traveling. Sometimes the drive takes five hours, or the flight three hours, and the distance can be in the thousands of miles. The distances are easily explained. Summer places near urban centers had been converted long ago into year-round dwellings, and as the country became suburbia, to get out even for a weekend meant major travel. Developers were buying up once-remote acreages and creating leisure villages of second homes. Buying has always been more important than renting to Americans, whether it's the home or the home away from home, even though the second home had many of the earmarks of neighborhood suburbia. In the late sixties builders turned out houses by the hundreds of thousands, and there was no shortage of buyers. In 1968 there were 1.7 million second homes in this country. By 1970, the figure was about 3 million, almost double the number in 1968. The total now must far exceed the 1970 figure.

For the most part, these second homes are just that—full-scale, year-round homes with plumbing, heating, electricity, suitable for use at any time during the year, and bought with an eye toward future full-time occupancy. Because there was now a place to get away to, the reasons for staying there increased, and weekends lengthened from Thursday to Monday. And sometimes a little in between. The shift has been subtle, but the transition from the midweek commuting to an apartment in town to the second home as the only house is becoming an increasingly popular way of life.

If the second home is a solution to staying in and surviving, it's also a psychological jolt that seems almost schizophrenic in its extremes of climate, topography, and life-style.

People leave San Francisco for their "cabin" on the Mendocino Coast or Lake Tahoe, three and a half traffic-laden hours away, and they call it a cabin whether it really is an old shack, a prefab A-frame, or an architect-designed custom house. Little communities develop extensions of the life they get away from—one for Stanford graduates only; another, The Lair of the Golden Bear, for Berkeley grads. The affluent doctors, dentists, and college professors turn from suave to grisly. It's planned roughing it—work shirts, Coleman lanterns, a deliberate attempt to escape the trappings of their affluent lives, if only for the weekend.

Even more extreme, leaving Los Angeles and five hours later being in a condominium in Maui or an open-deck house set into a slice of hill in Honolulu: from pin-striped suits to aloha shirts and designer dresses to muu-muus. People experience the extremes: rush and calm, civilization and the absence of it. In clothes, food, entertainment it's the leap from style to antistyle.

In the Midwest, north toward the Minnesota and Wisconsin trees and hills and away from the flatness that spells productivity. The quest is for all-day struggles with fish that fight like men, not men that work like fish.

In the East it's as easy to fly to a Cape Cod house as it is to drive a long-distance road to Vermont. More frequent these days are second houses in the Caribbean, where any cruel winter week can be traded in for the price of a ticket to ride south toward home. It's not at all unusual for working couples from New York and Boston or Cleveland and Detroit to spend many long weekends a year in the calmer waters.

It's not even odd anymore to hear of couples having second homes in England, France, Ireland, or even Spain. These are not just summer villas, hired out by the month, but weekend homes, with stays stretched sometimes to a week, but punctuated nevertheless by the regular workaday Stateside schedule. Talk about cultural shock. Let's say a couple lives in suburban New Jersey. On Friday night they take off, and after a seven-hour flight have picked up their little French car and are heading to their twelfth-century water mill outside of Paris. They might do their own cooking, shop the local markets, gorge on full, soft, fat cheeses and sweet young Beaujolais, probably never seeing another English-speaking person their whole stay.

However schizophrenic, a halfway house is probably better than staying in altogether. Unless it's so much like being home it seems like going nowhere. Weekend and vacation houses create their own work, sense of duty, social obligations. It's the same problem whether the halfway house is north or south from Los Angeles or Chicago. It's like the Hampton syndrome, for example:

Early in January, before they're even sure the summer is going to come, couples trek out of the city and, for many thousands of dollars, find a place to rent or buy on the eastern tip of Long Island. The season starts late in May and here is the usual relaxing procedure. In the middle of the week before every weekend, the discussion begins: "When do we leave on Friday? Right after work, or wait until after dinner?" The pros and cons of each alternative are scrupulously analyzed, as if the same discussion didn't take place each week. To leave as early as possible may mean you miss the paralyzing surge of traffic all heading in the same direction on Friday night. Sometimes it takes six hours. The other option, to have dinner in town and get there late, means, of course, that you get there late.

Imagine that for this weekend you've decided to stay in town and leave after dinner. Right away you start looking for a place to park the loaded car and not risk robbery, where you can have dinner and it won't take too long. If you wait till too late, you see, you'll run into the Long Island traffic *going home* from the Friday Night Theater in the city. Invariably, your predeparture dinner is rushed and tense. Then, once in the car, you tune in the road traffic reports, helicopter reports, boat reports, trying to get maximum input because now you have to figure out your route. Anyone who has driven this stretch several dozen times a summer and for repeated summers knows that you just don't get on the highway and go. That would be to miss the subtleties. There are fine and significant ways to decide what road to take. At every exit, at each major turn, there are many alternate ways to go. The options are appalling, gut-grinding, exhausting. When you finally do roll in around midnight, you're far too tired to so much as stop and breathe in some salty air. Your ears are still roaring from traffic, not the ocean.

The next morning, Saturday, you think you might just stay in bed awhile and let the sunny, soft summer air fill your room and your lungs. No way. You've got to get up and race right down to the tennis courts at daybreak to sign up for a court or you'll just never get to play all weekend, and what are you out here for, anyway? So you get there to find that some smart guy has come out on Thursday and reserved the court for the best times, the cool of the evening, and the only slots left are at three in the afternoon, which cuts into your beach time, and what are you here for, anyway? But you sign up.

Okay. Now to the Beach? Uh uh. You've got to race over to the IGA store before the milk and the chopped sirloin is gone for the weekend. You've got to stock up. Some couples refine the shopping strategy by doing it all in the city before they leave (trading money for time) or stop in at one of the big Long Island discount stores on the way (trading time for money). So you suburb-it-up at the supermarket and get back and put the stuff away and just as you finish that, why, of course, the weekend guests arrive. And are starving. So maybe around one o'clock you finally get to the beach, just in time to watch the sun go in forever over the six-foot-high waves breaking on the Atlantic shore. So you lie there in the semishade, cursing clouds, and who should come and sit right by you but your next-door neighbors from the city—one of the reasons you're here in the first place. And you listen while they tell you that you can get a bad burn on a day like today.

But that doesn't matter much because it's almost time to go back and change into tennis whites, and just as you arrive at the courts, the sun comes out brilliantly and defiantly. So you have your hour of sweaty running; then what, home for mint juleps? Uh uh. Still in your sweaty whites, more shopping. Because you haven't bought what you're out here for—fresh tomatoes and corn picked right from the stalk that you have to wait until the last minute to buy to get the freshest. So you head for the chic little roadside stand where lettuce costs about a dollar and where the produce comes from Florida and California for fully two-thirds of the summer season. Then it's off to the fish market to get a load of the just-out-of-the-water catch in from Montauk Point. At the fish market you run into your doctor and some people you met on the beach last year, all of whom ask you to cocktails, which you decline but feel guilty. And then you race home and wait itchily while your guests use the only shower before you, and by the time you get there there's no hot water in this charming beach house, and the tub has an inch of sand in it.

Then, of course, you've got to cook all the marvelous fresh food you bought, and dinners always take longer than they should. Right after dinner you're so tired you can't see straight, and everyone tells you it's the sun and the salt air.

All day Sunday is spent with necks crooked upwards, checking out the sky. Because if it's really going to stay as cloudy as it looks right now, you might as well beat the traffic and go back early.

The solution to second-home schizophrenia is, of course, to find a house where you make your own rituals, where there are fewer, or no people, or hand-picked friends. Finding a second house in the wrong place isn't helping you get out at all, because your main thrust is to substitute their rules for yours. If there are too many rules and if your neighbors' concerns are social, even in tranquillity, then there's no peace.

The best second-home situation I've ever observed

(short of that water mill in France, I mean) is a house in the north Georgia hills owned by five Atlanta couples: an architect, a graphic designer, a scaffolding salesman, an insurance entrepreneur, an Associated Press executive, and their wives of assorted talents. This is no group of disillusioned youngsters; many have kids of their own, and some of their kids have kids. They're all in their late forties or early fifties, living scattered over suburban Atlanta and were friends long before they started on the second-house venture. It was one of those open-ended conversations in someone's living room about one o'clock in the morning that finally delivered itself of a plan: they would find some land. The thought in back of some minds was to find a permanent retreat where they could open a shop or a restaurant together and send the confirmed newspaperman to the office every day on a motorcycle they'd buy him.

We've all had nights like those, where the "Why don't we's" and the "What about if we were to's" fill the air with promises. What was the difference? Maybe the time and stars were right. And the plan was small-scale to begin with. They dispatched each couple to a section of the state to check out their area and report what could be found. Several weeks later one couple discovered a venerable old house on over a hundred acres of rolling, woody land about two hours from the city. They all liked what they saw—a house that would be communal for a while, but with enough land to divide into five parts, one day, when enough ships would come in to build separate homes. So they joined in to float the loan and then, with respectable parliamentary procedure, they elected a president for a year and a treasurer and proceeded to collect seventy-five dollars a month for the mortgage payment, with a little left over for physical repairs.

Because it was an old chicken farm on a hill, it became Chicken Hill Ten, which was corrupted to Chicken Hilton. The wide wooden porch sags halfway round the house, hugging the coziness inside, immaculate with the joint efforts of five housewives. Each couple has its own bedroom. The architect dragged in an old stretch of fence, leaned it against his bedroom wall, and painted a rising sun on the wall behind it. The inveterate newspaperman started his own house organ, a bulletin-board gazette of the weekend's events wittily written in country style.

The group's organic garbage is composted in a pile out by the garden—unexpected munificence from the Georgia clay. Several of the more ardent farmers spend entire weekends on hands and knees.

The shared interest and, I guess, love of the group does away with the little arguments such groups are known for. "Everything is easier," one of the ten says. "I used to wonder what all these people were doing sitting on a porch and rocking all the time. Now when I get up here all I want to do is sit and rock. You can tell how long a person's been up here by how relaxed he is. You just ease into it. Everything's in slower motion."

Children come up but never sleep in the big house. Either they camp out or bunk in the house they're building from the old chicken coop. It really is the extended family. "There is a security of home you haven't had since you were a child," says the architect. "To me it's a psychological retreat. If I have a bad day and everything seems to go wrong, if I lose all this business, I say to myself, 'Well, I can always go live at the Chicken Hilton.' If anything ever happened to one of the husbands," he romanticizes, "we would take care of the wife, I mean in every way. If there is trouble or sickness, we would gather round. It's just natural to us now."

14

Travel Folders of the Movement

I am a 35-year-old corporation executive about to drop out of
the rat race, and I am looking for a companion for a 1972
canoe trip through Labrador. . . . Reader and admirer of Thoreau would be welcome.
                    Bill C., Brooklyn, N.Y., in *The Mother Earth News*

A sure sign that the idea of getting out is getting in to
one's consciousness is the amount of counterliterature
that can be found lying around desk tops and coffee tables. Counterliterature is distinguished by its assumption
that there is another way of living, characterized by the
catchphrases "counterculture" and "alternate life-styles."
These publications are often printed on recycled paper.
Their graphics are boldly black and white. You will
know them by their typographical errors and by their totally loving, committed, and enthusiastic endorsement of
this other way of living. Even if they're not quite sure
what it is yet.

For many who think about getting out, reading about
it is the first step. For others, reading is the only step, its
own kind of escape—getting out in your head. With a

gratification carried over from childhood cereal box tops, *sending away* is as good as doing it. Exotic counterpamphlets called *Land in the Ozarks, The Maine Idea, Australia, What's It Really Like?* Once you're into counterliterature, you'll find endless cross-references from editors eager to help each other along.

Many editors and writers in the counterliterature are refugees from the profit-grabbing, ad-kissing mentality of the big books, and they strive for honesty above all. Their prime motive is to spread the word—to open the Movement to those of its readers who are even slightly susceptible. They spend very few words reviling the establishment. They do not continuously put down the system they reject. They try to offer alternatives. In this way the counterliterature differs from the underground press: it is primarily nonpolitical, less self-serving, kinder to the language, and generally more professional. The underground press was the outgrowth of the political New Left in the late sixties. It existed to serve a clearly defined group of younger people alienated by the straight society. It existed to defend radical political tactics, drugs, rock music. It was the press of a violent time, and many of the newspapers once nurtured by the Liberation News Service have ceased to exist. In their place has come a press for our time—optimistic, exploratory, back to nature, a press that prints diagrams of yogurt makers instead of Molotov cocktails. It quotes Thoreau instead of Marcuse.

Because many of the writers of the counterliterature are out there living the new life, they become excellent sources for the slick press to report on the counterculture without going there itself. Ironically, the counterpress has an overwhelmingly generous attitude about sharing its material with its own compatriots in print; many encourage reprint without permission, which is even better for spreading the word. Instead of the factionalized competitiveness of the purely commercial press, counterpress members are each other's best fans.

The big daddy of the counterliterature was Stewart Brand's *Whole Earth Catalog*. With unusual publishing insight, Brand decided that just as there was a first catalog in 1968 (and published quarterly since), the last catalog would come in 1971, having printed all the news so fit. But the *Last Whole Earth Catalog* will be around for a long time. It so captured the public imagination in 1972 that it became a bestseller and won a National Book Award. The catalog describes itself with the modest subhead *Access to Tools*. There are tools between its outsize covers that astound: tools for the mind, the soul, the humanity of man. It's not the whole How-to but how to get to the right How-to. Every major book that ever had a word to say about the human condition pertinent to a counterlife is excerpted and reviewed. Every major tool is reviewed. Even reviews are reviewed. As the catalog says:

> The judgments in the reviews are wholly sincere. They are also only partially informed, often biased, very often wishful, occasionally a temporary enthusiasm. Many are simply hasty. I wouldn't rely on them too far. Try to see through them.

It occupies itself with the areas common to all counterliterature: the building and making of houses and shelters and everything to go in them, the growing and preparing and eating of food (organically, of course), nature and the complete enjoyment of it, medicine, crafts, animals, the arts.

Unlike the groups of self-righteous kids whose insistence on their way is so shortsighted it's bigotry, the catalog's bias is not to one life-style or one age group or one way of getting out. It is simply the most profound endorsement of the individual versus the system the twentieth century has seen:

> We are as gods and might as well get good at it. So far remotely done power and glory—as via government, big business, formal education, church— has succeeded to the point where gross defects obscure actual gains. In response to this dilemma and to these gains a realm of intimate, personal power is developing—power of the individual to conduct his own education, find his own inspiration, shape his own environment, and share his adventure with whoever is interested. Tools that aid this process are sought and promoted by the *WHOLE EARTH CATALOG*.

It's not a mystery then, when you see a suited-up executive carrying this black 11 × 14 manifesto under his arm. Alone in his office he can explore this "realm of intimate personal power." He can see how to set in floor joists of round logs before building a woodland shelter, and right away he is Robinson Crusoe constructing his fortress against the elements. He feels the need to confront himself with the realities of basic living, to use his strength just to survive. He can play with his fantasies. Or he can find out how to make a Buckminster Fullerlike dome in his backyard. Maybe he will walk out of his office and never come back. And maybe he won't. But books like the *Whole Earth Catalog* provide a bridge to a new way of looking at life.

Rolling Stone used to be in business just to perpetuate the rock-music industry, but it has become a far-reaching and incisive social commentator. Its audience is a mixture of hipster record promoters (Tin Pot Alley), kids, and straights. Although it is sustained by ads from the record industry, it is still the best interpreter of what the counterculture is about. "The state of the soul of the community is always calculable by the songs of the realm. . . ." writes *RS*'s philosophic columnist Ralph Gleason, out of the wisdom and sanity of a long time observing. As a newspaper, *Rolling Stone* is more in than gotten out and as such writes about outside from within. In the cooperative print spirit *Rolling Stone* early in the catalog's life printed whole spreads from the *Whole Earth Catalog* to give it a push.

The Mother Earth News in turn owes a lot to the catalog. Published bimonthly from what must be a very hectic place, Madison, Ohio, *TMEN* is a lively and responsible magazine dedicated to the practical ways of coping with another way of living. "It tells you how," is its motto, and inside are such articles as "How to Find and Finance a Farm," "Earn a Living in the Country," "Build a Home from Railroad Ties," "Power Your Car with Chicken Manure," "Raise Elk." The articles are written by random contributors, many of whom are out there living it. With *The Mother Earth News* and a long afternoon ahead of you, you can try on lives: on homesteads, in a yurt, in Canada. Reading the real-life stories of people of all ages who've gotten out is truly the great escape. You can see yourself out there struggling with a compost heap, sprouting beans, feeding five people breakfast for less than two cents. With every good intention, *TMEN* even publishes suggestions not too well tried, in hope that someone out there will. It describes itself as

> a bi-monthly publication edited by and for today's turned-on people of all ages. The creative ones. The doers. The folks who make it all happen. Heavy emphasis is placed on alternative lifestyles, ecology, working with nature and doing more with less.

Mother (who is in reality editor John Shuttleworth) has a happy sense of group effort about it. It suggests, helps, amuses, but never preaches, certainly a temptation for people so sure they're right. In every issue, pages and pages of letters are published from folks all over the country seeking information, help, land, friendship, family. It is a lonely heads' club. A way to communicate. The great reaction to this publication alone suggests the scope of the dissatisfaction, restlessness, and unfulfillment abroad in the land. With its latest issues, even *Mother* seems a little on edge, begging people not to crash its limited office space. The magazine is attempting to find some land and funds to start a research center to practice its alternate ideas, sounding not unlike the many classified ads it publishes: "For some time we've been thinking about buying several hundred acres in North Carolina or Virginia or Missouri or Arkansas . . ."

TMEN makes all its back issues available, so you can send for something you missed. Every issue is worth keep-

ing except one early issue called the "Have-More Plan,"
a homesteading package of practical advice about raising
goats; but it also had a lot about chemical fertilizers and
pesticides, which *TMEN* wouldn't be caught dead publishing today.

Dick Fairfield's *The Modern Utopian and Alternatives News-
magazine* is really a philosophical inquiry into the New
Life-Style writ in a light and incisive style (with colorful
and personal examples). One special three-in-one issue of
The Modern Utopian is called *Communes, USA* and is a book
rather than a magazine. With the kind of publishing phi-
lanthropism common to all the counterliterature, Dick
and company will not publish anything privately without
making sure it goes to all their subscribers as well. When
Penguin Books asked Fairfield to do a book on communes, he agreed, but insisted that it be sent first as a gift
to subscribers of *The Modern Utopian*. When asked to contribute a weekly letter to a group researching communes,
Fairfield also agreed, but only if his subscribers got a
copy too. So *Alternatives Newsletter* came about. This is
service publishing.

Communes, USA is as good a book on communal living
as has ever been written. A lot easier to get into and identify with than William Hedgepeth's beautiful but vague
and poetic picture book called *The Alternative*. Hedgepeth
makes it all sound like a hungry, barefooted, dusty
dream. Fairfield, just as earnestly searching out the answers, cuts through the mystique. He looks for the same
answers that people getting out seek. It is Fairfield who
points out the essentially bourgeois nature of communes
whose men grovel in the fields and whose women warm
the fieldstone hearth and bake dozens of loaves of bread a

day. He saw through religious-based groups who "publish the usual New Age religious bullshit about prophecy and abstract metaphysics." He is unimpressed by protestations of peace and love, showing realistically that communes, the successful ones, are at best neighborhoods of like-minded people who don't particularly welcome outsiders, be it reporters or casual passersby. But *The Modern Utopian* keeps searching in earnest for an alternative, and if this search takes us through many philosophical changes, all the better for choosing your own. Because Fairfield is still searching, we search with him. As he says in the introduction to still another book, *Modern Man in Search of Utopia*,

> this volume includes the visions and some of the practices of people who don't necessarily live in Utopia but they are certainly involved in the struggle. It is not meant to be escape literature, to make you feel good and then go on with your daily routine. On the other hand, it isn't meant to make you feel bad either. It is meant to stir you, to get you *involved*.

This is exactly what the counterliterature is about—the search.

Vocations for Social Change attempts to provide answers. Its self-declared purpose is straight enough:

> The primary function of *Vocations for Social Change* is to help people become involved in radically different work and lifestyles. This newsletter serves as a focal point for the dissemination of information

about available work/living opportunities which we have come across during our travels, readings and contacts with individuals and groups around the country.

VSC emphasizes ways to live in and out of the system with glorified and radicalized want ads. The rather stark typewritten format is surprisingly relieved by little drawings, quotes, and cartoons that show that no matter how intense and radical, these people don't take themselves too seriously.

In a well-meaning attempt to fill the vacuum left by the *Whole Earth Catalog* a number of new publications have emerged. *Organic Gardening and Farming*, Robert Rodale's excellent monthly, has come up with a one-time, one-dollar New York Metropolitan volume that tells you how to do it in the city. A new catalog-sized magazine called *Natural Life Styles—A Guide to Organic Living* is more related to food than any of the previous publications. With the wide-ranging naïveté typical of the counterpress, *Natural Life Styles* published a lot of doctors' theories on nourishment. The first issue is so down on milk it could turn you off Baskin-Robbins forever. *Natural Life Styles* print a lot of Euell Gibbons's foraging information, much of which is available in his well-known books, *Stalking the Healthful Herbs*, *Stalking the Wild Asparagus*, *Stalking the Good Life*.

Food and its preparation have always had strong cultural overtones, and the counterculture is not without its preconceptions of health food, or food not contaminated with the taint of the giant corporate food processors. Accordingly, endless natural-food cookbooks are being published that have housewives in suburban Boston warring for the first roadside lamb's-quarters and elderberries.

Books on farming at home or getting out to farm are appearing by the dozens, notably William Kaysing's *First-Time Farmer's Guide* and *How to Live in the New America*, which itself contains an endless list of special publications to help answer any question, find jobs and land, do all but push you out. Which gets back to the point— reading is just a substitute for doing.

The latest travel folder of the Movement is a magazine that deals squarely with getting out. It's called *Black Bart Brigade* and addresses itself directly to middle-class, middle-age discontent. Because the purpose of this book and *Black Bart Brigade* are so intertwined, it seems fitting that the one end with the statement of the other:

> We shall try to bring together those who have found better lives and those who would. The basic theme will be change by means of personal revolution, in values, goals and methods. The ones who have weathered the period of difficulty and uncertainty will share their knowledge and experiences, and the growing collection of resources: groups, publications, programs, etc., will be publicized and made known. In time, the accelerating movement for personal change will hasten the conversion of society as a whole to more human and equitable patterns of living and working.

Bibliography

Books

Bainbridge, John. *Another Way of Living: A Gallery of Americans Who Choose to Live in Europe.* New York: Holt, Rinehart & Winston, 1968.

Darlington, Jeanie. *Grow Your Own.* Berkeley: The Bookworks, 1970.

Defoe, Daniel. *Robinson Crusoe.* New York: New American Library of World Literature, 1961.

Fairfield, Richard. *Communes, Europe: Touring the Communal Life Styles of Europe.* San Francisco: Modern Utopian, Alternatives Foundation, 1972.

————. *Communes, USA.* San Francisco: Modern Utopian, Alternatives Foundation, 1971.

————, ed. *Utopia, USA: Writings on Contemporary Alternative Life Styles.* San Francisco: Modern Utopian, Alternatives Foundation, 1972.

Franke, David, and Franke, Holly. *Safe Places.* New Rochelle, New York: Arlington House, 1972.

Gallagher, Robert S. *"If I had it to do over again . . .": America's Adult Dropouts.* New York: E. P. Dutton & Co., 1969.

Gibbons, Euell. *Stalking the Wild Asparagus*. New York: David McKay Co., 1962.

Hawthorne, Nathaniel. *The Blithedale Romance*. New York: Random House, Modern Library, 1937.

Hedgepeth, William, and Stock, Dennis. *The Alternative: Communal Life in New America*. New York: The Macmillan Co., 1970.

Kaysing, William. *First-Time Farmer's Guide*. San Francisco: Straight Arrow Books, 1971.

————. *How to Live in the New America*. Englewood Cliffs, N.J.: Prentice-Hall, 1972.

Laurel, Alicia Bay. *Living on the Earth*. New York: Random House, 1970.

Linder, Staffan Burenstam. *The Harried Leisure Class*. New York: Columbia University Press, 1970.

Moral, Herbert R. *Buying Country Property*. Charlotte, Vermont: Garden Way Publishing Co., 1972.

Mungo, Raymond. *Total Loss Farm: A Year in the Life*. New York: E. P. Dutton & Co., 1970.

Nearing, Helen, and Nearing, Scott. *Living the Good Life: How to Live Sanely and Simply in a Troubled World*. New York: Schocken Books, 1970.

Price, Irving. *Buying Country Property: Pitfalls and Pleasures*. New York: Harper & Row, Publishers, 1972.

Reich, Charles A. *The Greening of America: How the Youth Revolution Is Trying to Make America Liveable*. New York: Random House, 1970.

Rimmer, Robert. *The Harrad Experiment*. New York: Bantam Books, 1967.

Skinner, B. F. *Walden Two*. New York: The Macmillan Co., 1948.

Thoreau, Henry David. *Walden*. New York: Doubleday & Company, Dolphin Books, 1960.

Wilson, Sloan. *Away from It All.* New York: G. P. Putnam's Sons, 1969.

Wouk, Herman. *Don't Stop the Carnival.* New York: Doubleday & Company, 1965.

Specialized Magazines

Black Bart Brigade. P.O. Box 48, Canyon, California 94516.

Last Whole Earth Catalog. Portola Institute, Random House (1971).

The Modern Utopian and *Alternatives Journal.* Published by Alternatives Foundation, P.O. Drawer A, Diamond Heights Station, San Francisco, California 94131.

The Mother Earth News. P.O. Box 38, Madison, Ohio 44057.

Natural Life Styles, Vol. 1 (1971). 53 Main Street, New Paltz, New York 12561.

Vocations for Social Change. Canyon, California 94516.